The Homeowner's Guide to MOLD

Michael Pugliese, CMR, CMT

RSMeans

The Homeowner's Guide *to* MOLD

- *Recognizing Mold & Its Hazards*
- *Removing Mold Safely & Effectively*
- *Maintenance & Construction Practices that Prevent Mold*

...plus an Insider's Guide to Mold Removal Contractors & Insurance Issues

Michael Pugliese, CMR, CMT

RSMeans

Copyright © 2006
Reed Construction Data, Inc.
Construction Publishers & Consultants
63 Smiths Lane
Kingston, MA 02364-0800
(781) 422-5000
www.rsmeans.com
RSMeans is a product line of Reed Construction Data

Managing Editor: Mary Greene. Editor: Andrea Sillah. Editorial Assistant: Jessica Deady. Production Manager: Michael Kokernak. Production Coordinator: Wayne Anderson. Composition: Paula Reale-Camelio. Proofreader: Jill Goodman. Book and cover design: Norman R. Forgit.

Printed in the United States of America

10   9   8   7   6   5   4   3

Library of Congress Catalog Number Pending

ISBN-13: 978-0-87629-821-3
ISBN-10: 0-87629-821-8

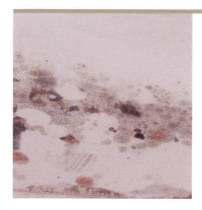

Table of Contents

About the Author & Reviewers

Michael A. Pugliese, author of this book, is a Certified Mold Remediator (CMR, Indoor Air Quality Association) and a Certified Mold Technician

(CMT, Association of Specialists in Cleaning & Restoration). He has spent thousands of hours over the past six years successfully cleaning up mold-contaminated environments. Many of his customers contracted his services after another remediator failed to get the job done right. He has performed mold remediation work for homeowners, corporate facility owners, major real estate companies, apartment communities, and insurance companies. His work has spanned eight states along the Gulf Coast and Eastern Seaboard, including major projects in the aftermath of Hurricane Katrina. Among Michael's clients are:

- Wachovia Bank
- Remax Realty
- Prudential Realty
- Travelers Insurance Company
- Cincinnati Insurance Company
- Fireman's Fund Insurance Company

Prior to his career as a mold remediator, Michael spent several years as a general contractor, where he acquired the skills needed to disassemble and rebuild components of a home contaminated with mold. He also has 13 years' experience working in the insurance industry, giving him a valuable perspective on handling mold claims. Visit the author's website at: **www.solutionstomold.com**

Reviewers of This Book

Gerry McGonagle is General Manager of A.R.S. Services in Newton, Massachusetts, a full-service disaster restoration firm in business for almost 20 years, and specializing in damage mitigation, mold remediation, property restoration, and disaster recovery services. The company is affiliated with numerous industry organizations, including the American Indoor Air Quality Council, National Association of Home Builders, National Association of the Remodeling Industry, and the Association of Specialists in Cleaning and Restoration.

Gerry holds the professional designations of Certified Restorer and Water Loss Specialist as certified by the Association of Specialists in Cleaning and Restoration (ASCR) and is also a Certified Mold Remediation Technician & Supervisor; Advanced Structural Drying Specialist; Fire, Smoke, and Water Damage Restoration Technician; and Mechanical Systems Hygiene Technician.

Howard Chandler is the Executive Officer of the Builders Association of Greater Boston, where he represents residential and light commercial builders throughout the region. He has spent more than 30 years in the construction industry, including building houses as the owner of a residential construction company, and as manager of field operations for a firm specializing in commercial, industrial, and institutional construction. In addition to his position with the Builders Association, Howard is a lecturer at Wentworth Institute of Technology in the construction management program.

Introduction

Why Is Mold Such a Concern Today?

Mold has been around since the beginning of time and is a natural component of life on earth … so why has it become such a big issue recently?

- The trend since the gas crisis of the 1970s has been toward "tight," energy-efficient houses with sealed openings to keep conditioned air inside, and outside air out. The problem is that any moisture generated or leaking inside is trapped there, providing ideal conditions for mold.

- Modern construction methods and materials like drywall and particleboard (with paper and cellulose) are a perfect breeding ground for mold, whereas older building materials, such as concrete and plaster, had greater resistance to mold growth.

- Increased remodeling of basements to expand living area has led to major mold problems when proper procedures were not taken to first prevent moisture from entering the space or to control the existing humidity.

- Well-publicized, high-dollar lawsuits have made people aware of the health and property damage risks and have caused insurance companies to reduce or eliminate coverage of mold-related damages.

- Recent weather disasters, such as the hurricanes in the Gulf Coast, have led to untold damage from mold growing in flooded homes.

Is Your House Making You Sick?

Imagine … every time you enter your home, you detect a strange or musty odor. You begin to have constant headaches and feel lethargic. Your children begin to run low-grade fevers and break out into rashes with off-and-on hay fever-like symptoms. The doctor has no specific diagnosis and tells you it may be allergies or "just the weather." These are the typical symptoms of a mold-contaminated house.

We've all seen the news about the multimillion-dollar lawsuits filed due to the adverse health effects of mold exposure. Mold is, in fact, classified by FEMA as a major hazard—along with natural disasters like hurricanes, tornadoes, floods, and fires. Mold has been linked to a range of illnesses, most often in children, the elderly, and people with allergies or compromised immune systems.

The most publicized mold is Stachybotrys, which has been linked to cancer and other adverse health effects. More common types, such as Aspergillus and Penicillium, can also be hazardous. These common molds typically grow outdoors, where they don't cause problems. But inside your house, in a high enough concentration, they can be harmful.

Protecting Your Home's Value

In addition to health risks, mold can have a major effect on your finances. For most people, their family home is the largest single investment they will ever make. How would you like to make the biggest purchase of your life and then find out it's neither livable nor sellable? Unfortunately, this has happened to a surprising number of American homeowners and homebuyers. The home of their dreams, whether their primary residence or a vacation or retirement home, turns out to be the largest financial mistake of their lives.

The owners of this relatively new home were surprised to find it was contaminated with mold, and shocked by the cost in time and money to fix the problem.

If a residence is severely mold-contaminated, it cannot be lived in or sold until the mold is remediated. Owners who have the financial resources will have to pay for the mold removal. If they cannot afford to finance the mold removal and do nothing about it, the home may have to be abandoned as unlivable shortly thereafter—and may be foreclosed on, possibly forcing the homeowner into bankruptcy.

Very often, home inspectors won't find mold during a home inspection. Some don't know exactly what to look for. In some cases, when homeowners discover mold in their homes after the purchase and seek a remedy—professional "mold remediation"—they're overwhelmed by the cost of the work, which, depending on the square footage of contamination, can range from a few thousand dollars to as much as $60,000 (or, in extreme cases, the cost to totally demolish and replace the structure). While total demolition is rare in mold situations, it's not uncommon for residential mold remediation costs to reach $20,000.

The mold remediation process can be elaborate and expensive. This home had to be gutted to remove mold-contaminated hardwood floors and wallboard. The subfloor and framing then had to be dried and treated to prevent the mold from regrowing.

As a Certified Mold Remediator (CMR) and a Certified Mold Technician (CMT), I have spent thousands of hours in mold-contaminated environments, performing successful mold remediations. Many of these situations could have been avoided altogether, or at least contained, by proper maintenance and timely repairs, better construction techniques and/or materials, or prompt identification and treatment of a mold problem. It's my hope that by sharing my knowledge and practical experience in this book, I can help families avoid having to suffer the negative health effects and financial losses associated with mold contamination.

How This Book Will Help You

In this book, you will learn about mold and its causes, the reasons why it is such an immediate and important concern, and the possible adverse health effects of mold exposure. I'll also explain how to detect mold in your prospective new home or current residence. One chapter gives you the basic principles on mold cleanup, so that whether you're able to do it yourself (for a small job), or have to hire a professional, you'll know what the goals are for a successful outcome.

Mold has been called "black gold" because the publicity about health risks and the need for remediation has attracted a lot of people to the mold remediation business. Since mold can occur in all regions of the U.S., and remediation can be expensive, many people who are not properly trained have jumped on the "mold bandwagon," only to discover that mold remediation can be a complicated, hazardous process. In fact, one-third of my business has been correcting work done poorly by "bandwagon mold remediators." That's why an entire chapter is dedicated to selecting a reputable mold remediator, should you need professional help. Along with the credentials you should look for, there are other tips for avoiding con artists and improperly trained contractors.

The book will also give you an overview of professional mold remediation methods so you'll know what to expect if you need this kind of work—and what's involved with mold testing—from kits you can purchase yourself to hiring an investigator.

The last two chapters focus on mold prevention. Chapter 10 is an overview of construction techniques that will minimize the chances of mold growing in your house. Whether you're having a new home built or planning a remodeling project, it pays to keep these principles in mind. This chapter includes an overview of the very latest construction materials specifically designed to prevent mold growth.

Chapter 11 lists important maintenance procedures that will not only help you keep mold out of your home, but extend the life of your appliances, air conditioning and heating systems, and flooring, windows, doors, and walls.

While mold can be a threat to your home and to your family's health, there is no reason to fear it. There are proven methods for successful mold removal and prevention. A common-sense approach and the guidelines in this book will help you recognize and avoid mold problems—and properly deal with mold if you do find it growing in your home.

Chapter

1

What Is Mold & Where Does It Come From?

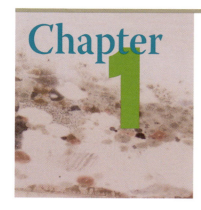

What Is Mold & Where Does It Come From?

Facts & Hype

There has been a lot of recent publicity surrounding mold, or, as the media has sensationalized it, "black" or "toxic mold." Multimillion-dollar lawsuits have brought about public awareness of the health hazards and property damage caused by mold. The fact is that mold has always been around and is a natural organism. Without certain types of mold, many of the things we enjoy and benefit from would not exist…such as penicillin, cheeses, yogurt, mushrooms, and an abundance of other things that we take for granted every day. In the wrong place and in excessive quantities, however, mold can be harmful—to homes, their contents, and their occupants.

Understanding How Mold Grows & Spreads

To successfully remove mold from your home, furnishings, and other belongings, you need to first understand what you're removing. If you need help from a professional mold remediation service, you'll want to have a sense of what those contractors are talking about when they explain the methods and processes they plan to use to eradicate the mold.

Mold is a member of the fungi kingdom, but it has physical characteristics of organisms in both the plant and animal kingdoms. While there are thousands of species of fungi, we normally deal with about 80 different species in the world of household mold remediation.

Stachybotrys (pronounced stacky-bot-tress)—or "black mold"—has been the subject of sensational headlines in the news, but the reality is that it's not as common in homes as many other species of fungi. The most common types of fungi collected in airborne samples in homes are Aspergillus, Penicillium, Ascospore, Basidiospore, Cladosporium, and Curvularia.

It's not easy to pull a dandelion up by the roots without disturbing the seeds on top. The same is true for fungi. When you're removing mold, the objective is to do so without causing it to lose any spores. Fungi/mold is spread through the release of spores. Once the mold spores have been disturbed, they become airborne, and if the conditions are right where they happen to land, they have a good chance of germinating and growing.

If you come across a moldy spot in your home, you'll notice that it seems to give off dust. That "dust" is actually mold spores, and by disturbing them, you're sending millions of them farther into your house, HVAC system, and furniture.

Mold is known as an opportunistic type of contaminant. Its spores can travel to neighboring rooms, land there, and not grow at all. They can sit there dormant for months or even years. Then one day the right combination of temperature and humidity will activate them, allowing them to germinate and start growing. That's why, during the remediation process, proper containment is a must to prevent cross-contamination.

Mold spores need a few things to grow:

- **Moisture**—which can come in the form of anything from humid air, to a dripping pipe, to major flooding.

- **Food**—material it can grow on, such as wood and wood products, paper, cotton, and leather. Mold will grow on anything where there is moisture and food, such as dirt or dust. (Mold has even been known to grow on steel doors, from the condensation that collects on them. When the condensation stops, the mold will stop growing and go dormant.)

- **The right temperature**—above freezing and below 120 degrees Fahrenheit. Summer-like temperatures, between 70–90 degrees, are especially conducive to mold growth. Freezing does not kill mold spores; it just makes them go dormant until temperatures warm up again.

Does My Home Have a Dangerous Type of Mold?

This is the number one question all mold remediators are asked. While Stachybotrys, or "black mold," has gotten a lot of publicity as a deadly substance, the fact is that many other molds are also toxigenic. Aspergillus, Penicillium, Ascospore, Basidiospore, Cladosporium, and Curvularia are all capable of producing mycotoxins/toxins. Some do turn black, but color alone is not an indication of toxicity.

Any type of mold can grow in large patches without producing any toxins at all. But if the mold becomes disturbed by temperature or humidity changes, that very same patch can begin to produce mycotoxins in the form of toxic spores and gases. The bottom line is that no mold growing in a home is good mold—period. After all, how many of your friends invite you over to their home to show off their mold?

To put it bluntly, if you have visible mold growth in your home, you need to have it removed. Whether the mold is white, black, green, maroon, turquoise, gold, or brown, it is still mold, and at some point it may produce spores or gases known to create adverse health conditions to human beings and pets.

All visible mold, not just black mold, could present a health hazard. It should be properly removed before it grows out of control.

"There Was Mold, but We Bleached It Out. Don't Worry!"

If you're considering buying a house, and the seller or builder says, "There was visible mold in the house, but we took care of the problem. We cleaned it up with bleach and painted over it," run, don't walk! This will not and does not work. More than likely, the mold will grow back through the paint in one to six months. The best remedy to properly correct this problem is to tear out all the contaminated drywall, remediate the areas, and replace the old drywall or other mold-contaminated materials with new ones.

Unlike man-made hazards like asbestos and lead, mold is a growing, living contaminant that, in excess quantities, can damage not only your health, but your home and its contents. Keeping mold in check means depriving it of the conditions it likes most—moisture and food (materials to grow on).

Whatever variety of mold you have, if it's visible or giving off a musty odor, it has to go. Mold cleanup or remediation must be complete, and the moisture source that caused the mold must be corrected.

Chapter 2

How Mold Can Affect Your Health

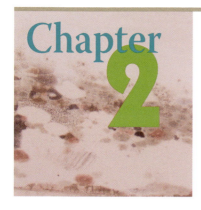

Chapter 2

How Mold Can Affect Your Health

Risks to People

The adverse health effects reported from mold exposure are wide-ranging in type and severity. Children, the elderly, and anyone with allergies or a compromised immune system are the most prone to illness from mold exposure. To put the allergy factor in perspective, one out of five people are said to suffer from allergies or asthma. The Asthma & Allergy Foundation ranks these conditions as the sixth leading cause of chronic disease in the U.S.

The most common effects of mold exposure are respiratory ailments including exacerbated asthma, shortness of breath, wheezing, and lung irritation. The presence of mold can also cause:

- Sinus problems, such as sneezing and runny nose
- Burning or itchy eyes
- Nervous system problems, such as headaches and tremors
- Depression and memory loss
- Fatigue, lack of energy
- Dizziness
- Nausea, digestive problems
- Low-grade fever
- Skin rashes, itching, welts, or hives
- Changes or suppression of immune system (increased susceptibility to disease)

More severe ailments that have been linked to mold toxicity include various forms of lung disease and cancer. Since fungi, like humans, have DNA, testing methods are now being developed to track and identify specific fungi and the true physical damage they can cause to the human body.

Complicating reactions to mold exposure is the sensitivity many people have to mold-eating mites—microscopic insects that are attracted to mold by the chemicals it releases. (The same chemicals are also the source of the musty smell.) People with multiple sensitivities may have to sort out which of the many possible indoor pollutants are causing their symptoms. These may include "off-gassing" from new carpet, paint, and furnishings; chemicals in cleaning products; aerosol sprays; smoke; pet dander; and insect droppings; in addition to allergies they may have to food and medications.

Risks to Pets

It has been shown that dogs, cats, birds, and other pets also have a sensitivity to mold toxicity and may suffer effects similar to those experienced by people. Field exposure of animals to molds shows effects including increased susceptibility to infectious diseases that can harm the intestinal tract, skin, or lungs, depending on how and what parts of the body were exposed. If the respiratory tract is affected, bacteria or viruses may not be as easily cleared, and there may be a greater susceptibility to cancer.[1]

Interestingly, dogs have been trained to sniff out mold in homes, although many in the mold remediation field might challenge the accuracy and consistency of this method. The variables include the many different types of fungi, each of which may have its own smell.

The Infamous "Black Mold"

Stachybotrys has been the headliner in most of the major mold lawsuits publicized in the media. It is slow-growing and takes longer to incubate than most fungi. It does not compete well with other faster-growing fungi and is rarely found in the outside natural environment. This fungus has been documented to emit trichothecene mycotoxin satratoxin-H, which, if inhaled, is poisonous. Stachybotrys grows on drywall and other cellulose products. People exposed to this fungus have reported:

- Flu- and cold-like symptoms
- Diarrhea
- Sore throats
- Headache

1. http://www.mold-help.org/content/view/457/

Stachybotrys growing behind a leaking refrigerator.

- Fatigue

- Skin rashes

- Hair loss

- Liver and kidney cancer

- Bone marrow and lymphoid disorders

- Lung cancer

Stachybotrys spores have been recorded as toxigenic, and this fungus should be treated with caution.

(See Appendix B for more detail on the health problems associated with several other specific types of common household molds.)

How Mold Gets Into Our Bodies

Mold can access and irritate people and animals in a variety of ways. We inhale mold spores into our lungs when we breathe. This is why it's important to use proper protection when you clean up even relatively minor patches of mold—and why those who are sensitive to it should not perform this task.

Mold can also get on our skin, where it may not cause a direct problem, but if you touch your face with mold-contaminated hands, you may inhale or swallow the spores or get them in your eyes or ears.

Increasing numbers of contact lens wearers have reported going back to wearing eyeglasses after contracting a fungal infection called Fusarium keratitis in their eyes through the use of contact lenses. These infections have so far been reported in more than one third of the United States, and are a growing problem. Fusarium is commonly found in plant material and soil. If the infected person does not receive the proper eye-drop treatment, which may take up to two to three months, the infection can scar the cornea.

Fungal skin infections have become more common as well. Athlete's foot is the most common, but other skin fungal infections are on the rise. Normally, they're treated with one of several topical anti-fungal creams, although in some cases, systemic treatments are prescribed.

Mold has been classified by FEMA as a major hazard and linked to many health problems—from frequent allergy symptoms to much more serious effects. Homeowners need to learn how to prevent mold, how to recognize mold if and when it's already growing, and what needs to be done to get rid of it and stop it from coming back.

The remaining chapters of this book will show you what to do at every phase: inspecting/testing for mold and getting rid of it; mold prevention tips when you're building a new home or remodeling; and maintenance steps to keep mold away.

1. http://www.mold-help.org/content/view/457/

Chapter 3

Does Your Home (or One You Plan to Purchase) Have Mold?

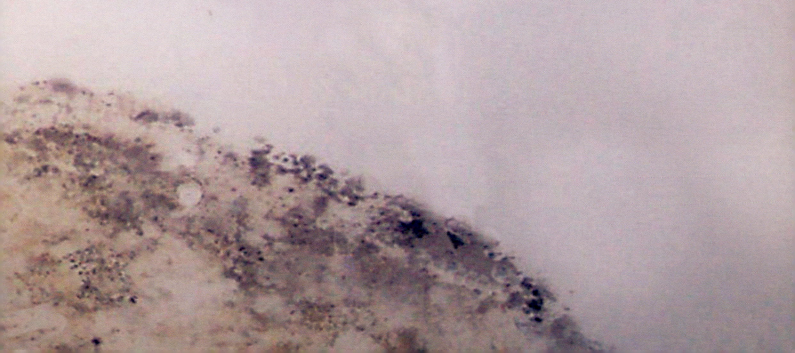

Chapter 3

Does Your Home
(or One You Plan to Purchase)
Have Mold?

Looking for Mold

Mold, like anything else, is easy to locate if you know what to look for and the right questions to ask. Some good general indicators include:

- A musty smell. (Approximately 90% of the homes with mold have this.)
- Evidence of a water leak or condensation.

Asking the Right Questions

If you're purchasing a new home, you have a right to know if there has been flooding or water damage to it, if mold testing has been done, or if any significant structural repairs have been made. You can ask your real estate agent to include a statement requiring full disclosure of these items in your contract. If the seller is available, you have a great advantage, as you can ask questions and get more specific information.

Whether you're buying a house or currently own a home and are concerned about mold, ask the seller (or yourself) the following questions. Then use the water inspection guidelines recommended later in this chapter to conduct your own inspection for possible water damage and mold.

- What is the condition of your roof? How old is it? If it's been replaced, when? Has it ever been patched? If there was a problem, do you know how long the roof had been leaking? (If the roof was replaced or patched, it was most likely because it was leaking, which may have resulted in some damage. You'll need to get a good flashlight and examine the attic using the procedures detailed later in this chapter.)
- Have you had chimney, dormer, vent pipe, or other flashing repairs done?

- Have you had window casings or trim replaced?
- Have you had any repairs made to your siding?
- Have you ever replaced the hot water heater? When? Was it due to a leak? How long did it leak before it was replaced? (According to insurance company reports, water heater leaks are one of the three top causes of water damage.)
- How is your air conditioning unit functioning? Have you ever had the condensation line/pump back up? (If the air conditioning condensation pump has been replaced, this was probably because it failed and leaked. Another source of leaks is the condensate drip pan. You'll need to examine its surrounding area and the materials underneath: basement, crawlspace, or the ceilings of the rooms below.)
- Is the heating and/or central air conditioning system in the crawlspace or attic? If in the attic, has it ever leaked onto the attic floor or ceiling below?

Why It's Important to Know if There Is Mold in a Home You May Be Purchasing

Mold is found in homes much more often than you would imagine. A typical pre-purchase home inspection is limited to visible mold and guidance on what needs to be done to correct it. But, in some cases, an indoor environmental/mold professional may be called in to test for mold. Many times, to the dismay of the seller, the buyer, and the real estate agent, mold inspection reports have ended negotiations for a home's sale.

If you own a home that's already contaminated by mold, that's one thing, and by now you know remediation is in order. But if you're purchasing a home, make sure any mold problems are corrected beforehand. Keep in mind, mold remediation can cost many thousands of dollars.

In addition to the remediation expense, you may have additional costs for alternate housing, since in many cases, you can't stay in the house during the remediation. The process can take from one to ten weeks, and is only the first phase. After the remediation is completed, the home then must be restored and/or repaired. This may include replacing drywall, insulation, tile, subflooring, baseboards and other molding, carpeting, cabinetry, ductwork, and whatever else was removed during the remediation process, plus painting.

Always take into consideration that there is a cost for the mold remediation and a separate cost to have your home restored to livable condition. And of course, along with the cost comes the time it takes for both of these tasks.

Other Critical Questions

- Has the dishwasher ever overflowed?
- Have any of the sinks or toilets leaked?
- Has the refrigerator or icemaker ever leaked water?
- Has the washing machine ever leaked, backed-up, or overflowed? (Like hot water heater leaks, washing machine leaks are among the top causes of water damage.)
- Have you ever had sewage back up?
- Have you ever had a broken pipe anywhere in the house?
- Have you ever had groundwater from the outside of the house run into or under the house?
- Have you had any problems with moisture in your crawlspace?
- Have you replaced the shower unit or tile? (Shower leaks share top billing for causes of water damage.)

If you're the homeowner and have owned your home for a while, you should be able to answer all of the above questions. If you're buying a house, an honest seller will be your best source of information. Since most homeowners typically know very little about mold, they may have no idea why you're asking so many questions about water leaks. If you do learn of a water leak and its location, you now know where to begin your mold investigation.

When purchasing a home, it's highly recommended that you include in the home sales contract a notation that the seller must disclose the name of their insurance company and policy number, along with the property disclosure statement. A signed consent form enabling the insurance company to release any and all claim information to you may be required.

When the Seller or Property History Is Not Available

Many times, the homeowner or seller will not be available to answer your questions, and little or no past property history may be found. Become a water detective! Again, this is not as difficult as you might think. Look for clues to detect water problems in the home.

Water Inspection Guidelines

To get an initial sense of whether there's mold in the home and where the problems lie, you can do your own investigation using the following guidelines. If you suspect that mold is present—based on a musty smell and/or obvious signs of water stains and leaks—you should wear at least a minimal-protection breathing mask (NIOSH N95), which you can purchase at a home center. If you know you're mold-sensitive or are prone to allergies, it's best to have someone else do this inspection. If you can inspect the property after or during a heavy rain, you'll be able to see existing leaks that may be coming through the roof, siding, doors, window frames/sills, crawlspace, or basement.

Ceilings & Walls

Check every corner of every room at the ceiling level and down the corner of the wall to the floor. A brown stain (similar to the color of a wet tea bag) and/or blistering of wallpaper and wallboard are what you're looking for. If staining or blistering are found in the upper level of a home, it most likely indicates a roof leak, but it could also be caused by an HVAC condensation line backup or a rotted dormer.

If found on the first floor, ceiling leaks may be from a bathroom pipe above. These stains may also indicate either an internal plumbing leak or roof leak that has been redirected from the original source. This can

This roof leak stained the ceiling. The entire attic above was found covered in mold.

happen, for example, when water from a tub or shower leak runs down a floor joist into another room before it begins to pool, becomes wet, and forms a stain.

If the stains are in the upper-level ceiling or corners of the home, examine the attic or the floor above the stained area. Check all roof areas for newly installed wood, wetness, or dried water-stained areas. Also check the area around the furnace and central air conditioning systems.

If a water stain is found on a ceiling (with no attic access) or wall, an exploratory hole must be cut through the drywall. The hole must be large enough to properly examine the inside cavity. This drastic measure is the only way to ensure that the water leak has stopped and that no mold growth is present.

If you hire a professional to assess the property, he can drill a smaller hole to test behind the wall with a probe, causing less damage to the wall. Keep in mind that there may be asbestos in the wall or insulation materials, and you must take precautions to avoid breathing in any disturbed particles of these hazardous materials.

An exploratory hole cut at the site of a ceiling stain reveals the mold growth hidden on the joists above.

Also check closets that are on outside walls. Sometimes these spaces are under-insulated or not insulated at all, and with their doors closed to the adjacent room, can be very cold in winter. That difference in temperature from the conditioned air in the house can lead to condensation and mold, especially in corners, near the floor, and on items stored in the closet. See "Bathroom Walls" later in this chapter for more on what to look for.

Hardwood Floors

Hardwood floors can provide you with a good history of previous water damage. If the kitchen floor is hardwood, examine it carefully, especially in front of the refrigerator, sink, and dishwasher, as well as along windows and exterior doors. Any discoloration or cupping of the floor can indicate

This hardwood flooring was on a kitchen floor in front of the refrigerator. Notice the separated seams in the wood, the cracks and bubbles in the polyurethane finish, and the wood discoloration. Water damage like this is an indication that mold could be present.

a water leak. (Cupping occurs when the edges of the hardwood strips are higher than the centers, or "curl up.") Also pay attention to the finish of the floor, as it may have different or faded coloration indicating water damage. If you believe the floor has been damaged, it's important to examine the ceilings in the space or rooms below the leak area as well.

Vinyl Flooring

The condition of vinyl flooring can also be a good indicator of water damage. Examine the baseboards in the kitchen, under the cabinet areas, and behind the refrigerator. When vinyl flooring is damaged by water, it usually separates from the shoe or baseboard molding and the cabinetry.

Doors & Windows

The casing or trim molding surrounding doors and windows of a home can tell the story of water damage. Two of the most common indicators are bubbled-up or peeling paint and a brownish stain. Darkened wood along the inside edge of sliding glass or French doors may indicate water leaks and mold growth from rainwater splashing from the roof and into the door frame/track. If you see rot, that means there has been long-term water damage and a greater chance of finding mold underneath. If there is carpeting, you may have to pull it back to see the damage below. Also check the ceiling in the space below for leaks and mold.

A window leak and the resulting mold growth hidden behind the baseboard.

Hot Water Heater

Check the manufacture date on the hot water heater label. If it doesn't coincide with the original building date of the home, it has been replaced. Water heaters are typically replaced because they've rusted out and leaked. You need to look at the hot water heater, surrounding walls and flooring,

Mold growth caused by a hot water heater leak in the basement of a home.

and the area of the house under the hot water heater, e.g., the basement, crawlspace, or the ceilings of the rooms below.

Check to see if the baseboards near the water heater are cracked or separated from the walls or coming apart at the mitered joints. If so, you'll want to remove the baseboards to see if mold has grown on or behind them and on the drywall. Also, if the hot water heater is on a vinyl floor and the vinyl flooring edges have curled up and pulled away from the baseboards, you'll need to pull back the vinyl and check the baseboard and subflooring for mold growth.

Sinks

Carefully examine the area under every sink in the home. Look for water stains under the pipes. If the sink cabinets are made of particleboard, you'll see a swelling or discoloration of the wood under the pipes if a water leak has occurred. If you see evidence of water leaks, you'll want to remove

Black mold growing directly out of the joint of a sink. Since most bathroom and kitchen cabinets are hollow underneath, check for signs of moisture on the cabinet floor. Any indication of water should raise suspicions.

the cabinet flooring to examine the extent of the damage and find out if mold is growing under the hollow part of the cabinets.

You can check the ceiling of the room, basement, or crawlspace below the sink for evidence of leaks. You can also test for leaks by filling the sink and then draining it, watching the pipes below. Kitchen sinks may leak from spray hoses as well as faucets and drains.

Showers & Tub Surrounds

Underside of cracked, leaking shower pan.

In addition to possible sink leaks, bathrooms are prone to shower leaks. Inspect for cracks and missing grout and caulk between tiles and/or a shower and tub. Showers and shower pan leaks are common sources of water problems and mold growth.

Toilets

Toilet leaks are frequently responsible for mold problems. Often a broken or cracked elbow joint just below the toilet or a toilet flush overflow are the culprits for toilet leaks causing mold. Sewer backups are probably the number one mold problem connected with this bathroom fixture. When a sewer backs up, make sure the water extraction company treats for bacteria, viruses, and fungal contaminants, as this "black water" is full of contaminants that are hazardous to your health.

Bathroom Walls

Bathroom walls can also collect mold unless they are properly maintained and ventilated. Unless there's a very good ventilation system/operable window(s), you have an increased chance of mold growth. Isolated mold, as in the folds of a vinyl shower curtain, can cause a musty odor. This is easy to fix by containing the curtain in a plastic garbage bag to avoid spreading the mold spores, throwing it out, and replacing it.

Laundry Rooms

A washing machine overflow resulted in mold growth.

Laundry rooms are notorious for water leaks. Check for evidence of previous water leaks in the same manner recommended for the room containing the hot water heater. Leaking washing machine hoses are one of the most frequent sources of water damage. Unless you turn the water off at the shut-off valve when the machine is not in use, there is pressurized water in the hose all the time. If hoses are not installed properly or are knocked off the drain, there are problems. When installed, there should be no kinks or tight bends in the hose, and there should be a minimum of 4˝ between the back of the machine and the water source. Steel braided hoses are recommended.

Heating, Ventilation, & Air Conditioning (HVAC) Systems

Examine all HVAC registers in the home. (These are the air vents used to distribute and enable air flow for cooling and heating the home.) Open and close each register, and examine both sides of the vent openings. If black

material is present on the register covers, this could indicate a mold problem. Black material could also be attributed to soil filtration from a poorly maintained system, oil burner malfunction, or soot residue.

Many people mistakenly believe mold growth on air vents like this to be simply dust or dirt. When you see this type of material, examine all HVAC registers thoroughly.

Ductwork can harbor mold when dust collects and poorly-insulated ducts accumulate condensed moisture. If air from the HVAC system smells musty, there is likely to be fungal growth in the ductwork, requiring professional cleaning and, in some cases, replacement.

Check all HVAC flex ducts in the basement, attic, and crawlspace areas. Mold will grow directly on the insulation and on the foil covering of the HVAC flex ductwork. Also examine the condensation line coming from the HVAC unit and all areas close to it.

With air conditioning, the condensate pan may overflow when the drain becomes clogged. An overflow tray with a floating shut-down switch can prevent this problem.

It's very important to examine the HVAC unit regardless of its location. Units may be located in the attic, crawlspace, or in two or more areas if the home has more than one system.

Having the right HVAC system for a finished basement is crucial to maintaining an environment that will not encourage mold. Often people are chiefly concerned about the look of their new basement living space and will cut corners on the HVAC unit due to the cost. The correct HVAC

Mold is detected on the PVC condensation line leading out of the HVAC system.

system for a finished basement can be costly—about $3,000–$5,000. Trying to feed the new space off an existing HVAC unit can be a considerable savings to a remodeling budget—but these savings may be costly.

Unfinished Basements

Basements are a prime area for mold growth and should be examined very carefully. First, closely check the pipes that pass through the basement ceiling from the floor above. Look around each pipe for indications of old leaks, such as wood discoloration or stains on the basement floor. Unusual discoloration of the wood surrounding any plumbing indicates a water problem.

Interior sump-pump drains are somewhat of an open invitation for mold—something to consider if there's one in a house you're thinking of purchasing. In some cases the problem that required the pump can be solved by re-grading the slope of the land to prevent water running into the basement. But if the problem is that the lot is in a high water table area, there may not be a good solution.

While the presence of a sump-pump collection area isn't proof of chronic moisture problems, many of these pumps are seated in wet wells (basically water in a hole), and that moisture increases the chances of mold. If the hole is dry when you see it, and it's intended to deal with any water intrusion from an occasional disaster, such as minor flooding associated with a hurricane, there may not be a big problem—but it does indicate that there was a previous water problem. As a potential buyer, you'll want to ask when water last got in so you know what kinds of conditions can be expected to result in water intrusion.

Discolored floorboards and joists are clear evidence of a moisture, and possibly mold, problem.

It is important to inspect each floor joist, as some—like this one—may have visible mold, while others around them appear clean.

Examine the floor joists that support the house and floor above the basement. Follow each joist its entire length and width, looking for wood discoloration running down or even parallel to the top part of the joists. If there is discoloration, a water leak has most likely occurred at some time. Check each framing member. Just because there is no mold growth on one does not mean there is no mold growth in other areas. In fact, it's common for an isolated wood beam to have some visible mold growth, while those

Water stains on basement walls and floors are usually easy to see and difficult to hide.

directly next to it look entirely clean. Structural wood as much as 25' away from the first mold sighting may be heavily coated with mold.

Examine all basement walls and the entire floor. Moisture is easily detected in cinderblock and concrete floors. If the basement floor has water stains, or if the walls are excessively damp, the cause must be determined. Most leaks are due to groundwater seeping in from the outside. Make a mental note of the location of the water stains, and head outside to examine these exterior areas of the home. Gutter drainage problems are the cause 75% of the time. The other 25% is usually due to a negative ground slope, directing the groundwater toward the home instead of away from it.

Finished Basements

When basements are finished with carpeting, paneling, and other materials, inspecting for mold can be more complicated because the signs are hidden. The first clue is a musty smell. If unwanted water or water vapor has entered the space, mold spores may be growing, fed by everything from carpets and wall paneling or drywall to wood or upholstered furniture, cushions, curtains, and anything else stored in the area.

Carpeting should be carefully considered on basement floors. A synthetic carpet with a porous carpet pad offers the advantage of allowing moisture vapor to migrate through and into the air where it can be processed (e.g., by a dehumidifier) or ventilated. The problem with carpet in a basement is that organic materials eventually settle in the carpet and act as a food source for mold when the moisture level rises enough for mold growth to occur.

Vinyl flooring or resilient tile is durable and can be cleaned more easily, but it also acts as a vapor barrier when placed over a concrete slab. Typically, a concrete slab will have consistent vapor pressure trying to migrate out of the concrete into the drier surrounding air.

Crawlspaces

Mold growth on the floor joists in a crawlspace.

Crawlspaces are notorious for mold growth. These areas are usually hard to access and evaluate since they tend to be very damp, cramped, and, like attics, are neither really inside nor outside.

The crawlspace inspection is a combination of basement and attic inspection procedures.

- Look for groundwater leaks.
- Look for wall leaks and dampness.
- Look for overhead leaking pipes.
- Examine the HVAC unit carefully, if one is present.
- Inspect all framing members for visible mold growth.
- Look for a vapor barrier over the soil.

If mold is present in these spaces, the materials that it's growing on should be replaced or thoroughly cleaned to remove the mold spores. Dirt floors should be covered by a heavy-duty vapor-barrier material.

Wood rafters in an attic with gray mold growing on them.

Attics

Attics are another place where mold growth is frequently found. Poor ventilation, roof leaks, and HVAC problems are usually the cause. In most attics, there's an abundance of exposed wood and insulation on which mold can grow. (The fiberglass material in the insulation does not support mold growth, but the paper backing does.)

Attics, like crawlspaces, are somewhat tricky to work with, as they're neither fully inside nor outside due to the nature of their construction, openness, and ventilation. An attic inspection should be performed in much the same manner as a basement inspection. Instead of looking for ceiling pipe leaks, you need to look for roof leaks.

Roof leaks can be caused by anything from damaged shingles to improper flashing installation around chimneys, exhaust pipes, and dormers. Flat roofs have their own issues because they lack the advantage of a clear slope to shed water. Sometimes gable-type sloping roofs collect mold on their lower edges, especially on the north side of the house, where the sun doesn't have as much opportunity to dry the wood out after a rain.

Although you probably won't see any related damage in the attic, you should also check the condition of the home's gutters and downspouts from the outside, as they're roof items that are key to avoiding water intrusion into the house.

Examine the area around all vents, as well as all roof decking, rafters, and attic floor joists. Check all penetrations including chimneys and pipes going up through the roof to exhaust furnaces, the hot water heater, plumbing, fireplaces, etc.

Dryer and bathroom exhaust systems should never be vented into the attic, as this will cause condensation—and mold. Make sure there are no sources of moisture from the living space to the attic above. Proper attic vents to the outdoors are also important.

Inspecting the insulation can be a bit of a challenge. Roll insulation usually shows water stains on the paper backing, which will speed up your water leak investigation … but blown-in insulation is harder to inspect because it hides the water stains. You have to move the blown-in insulation to expose the surface underneath it to find the water stains. Be sure to also closely inspect any HVAC unit(s) and carefully examine the areas around them.

Attic sheathing or rafters damaged by mold growth may need replacement in cases of severe mold infestation, but this is typically a last resort.

Finished attics have the same inspection challenges as finished basements—evidence of mold may be covered by carpeting or wall finishes.

Also refer to the heating, ventilation, and air conditioning systems guidance earlier in this chapter for more on the causes of mold and what to look for in attics.

Mold on the Home's Exterior

Often in humid climates, a substance that looks like mold will grow on roofs and siding. It could be mold or mildew, but it could also be algae or moss—which start out green, then typically turn brown as they dry, then black as they age.

Cleanup can be done by pressure-washing (or washing with a stiff brush) using a good detergent that will not harm the environment. If there is mold, moss, or algae on your roof or siding near any entry points, such as doors and windows, clean it up and check that area regularly to make sure the growth does not come back. If you're pressure-washing, plan this job for a time when the forecast promises a few hot, dry days to follow.

A pre-purchase inspection for mold should be as compulsory as a standard home inspection prior to the sale. While a broken air conditioner or hot water heater can be an unplanned expense, it won't make your family sick the way mold can. If your home suffers a water leak, repair it. Then, each day after the drying-out has been performed, for a period of two weeks, it is highly advisable to check the affected area daily for any type of mold activity. After two weeks, if no mold activity is visible, chances are the dry-out was performed correctly and you shouldn't have a mold problem.

Chapter
4
Mold Testing

Chapter 4

Mold Testing

After Your Inspection

After your visual inspection for water damage and mold is complete, you have either discovered mold or found no visible signs of it. You may now choose to:

- Do nothing further if you've found no visible signs or musty smell.
- Confirm your suspicions of mold contamination with lab testing.
- Get a second opinion from a mold remediation/testing professional.
- Have mold testing performed to provide contamination proof for a third party, such as a buyer or insurer.
- If the only mold you find is a small problem, like a moldy shower or tub, clean it and maintain the area to keep it mold-free.

When you see visible mold growing in your home, there's usually no need to test it unless you just want to know what type of mold you have. By most standards, this is a fairly worthless test. It's analogous to seeing a person lying in the street bleeding; there would be little need to ask if anything was wrong. Clearly this person needs help! The same goes for mold in your home. If you see it growing, it really doesn't matter what kind it is … you still need to have it removed.

If you have discovered mold, there are some cases when you would want to test it prior to any remediation work. Some of the reasons:

- Proof for an insurance company
- Proof for a lawsuit
- Proof for a seller
- Conclusive reporting and evidence when no visible mold has been detected, but someone in the house has symptoms

- To provide a baseline measurement to compare to final clearance testing to indicate successful removal to a "normal condition"

If You're Considering Mold Testing

Collecting mold spore samples, regardless of the type, is not a tremendously difficult task. You may have the most efficient spore collector in the galaxy working for you, but the results will only be as good as the microbiology laboratory that analyzes the samples.

As a result of all the attention mold has received recently, there are not only "bandwagon remediators," but "bandwagon testing laboratories." Many material laboratories that previously performed metal and asbestos testing are now getting into the mold spore counting business. You need to confirm the laboratory's credibility by asking the following:

- Exactly what laboratory will analyze the spore samples from your home?
- Does this laboratory have a full-time microbiologist on staff? What are his/her credentials?
- Is the laboratory certified? If so, by whom?
- What process is used to actually count the spores?
- How long has the laboratory been performing mold spore count tests?

The person collecting the mold spore samples from your home should be able to answer all of these questions. If he or she cannot, be wary.

Before Testing

If the air conditioning or heat had been running during the time of suspected contamination, then testing should be done with the same units running. Shut all windows and doors 24 hours prior to testing to get a true mold spore count in the house. Try to let the house sit for a 24-hour period without a lot of people going in and out, reducing the traffic and number of times the doors open and close. The key is to test the normal environment that you're living in.

The Home Test Kit

If you wish to spare the expense of having a certified mold specialist perform your inspection and mold spore sampling, you can purchase a mold home test kit from your local hardware store or home center. These kits generally cost about $10 to $15, with an additional charge to send the petri dish to the laboratory for a mold spore analysis and report.

All in all, these kits are easy to use. Keep in mind that if you're interested in an exact identification of the types of mold you're dealing with, you might want to hire a certified Indoor Environmental Professional with the skills and experience to collect and evaluate spore samples with precision.

Types of Mold Spore Testing

There are several types of mold spore tests available. They use different methodologies, and there are different reasons for using each type.

Swab Test

The swab test is exactly that—use of a cotton or material swab to wipe the surface to be tested. This is a common practice for testing areas such

as air ducts and can be used on almost any surface. After touching one to three surfaces in the same location, the swab is sealed in a container and sent to the microbiology laboratory for examination. Swab testing is generally used to detect mold and to determine what types of mold are present. This test is not typically designed to identify mold spore counts.

Swab sample being taken.

Tape Slide Test

Tape slide tests are similar to swab tests. A piece of tape is placed onto

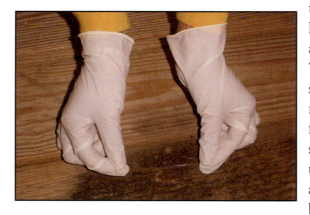

the area to be tested, lifted, and placed onto a glass microslide. The tape slide is then sealed and sent to the microbiology laboratory for examination. Tape slide testing is generally used to detect mold, and the same tape may be applied to several locations, such as a wall, a sofa, and the underside of a table, depending on what the person conducting the test is looking for.

Tape slide sample being taken.

Tape slides also determine what types of mold are present. Like the swab test, tape slides are not typically used for mold spore counts.

Petri Dish Testing

Petri dish testing is used for several different purposes. The dish may be placed in a room for several minutes to passively collect airborne particles, including any mold spores that may be present. The dish may also be

This petri dish from a home test kit was left open for ten minutes in what was believed to be a slightly mold-contaminated room. These mold spores cultivated without the help of an incubator in a 48-hour period in the client's home. This home sample clearly shows significant mold growth.

placed into a cylinder that forces air over the exposed dish. This process collects mold spores and atmospheric particles more rapidly. In both processes, the petri dish is then covered and usually sent to the microbiology laboratory for testing.

The laboratory then incubates or grows cultures in the dish to determine if *viable*, or living, mold spores are present, the type of mold, and if harmful toxins are being produced.

Mold Spore Trap Testing

Mold spore trap testing is probably the most widely used method of mold spore detection. The spore trap is an actual microslide fitted with a collar to hook directly to a vacuum pump. The pump pulls cubic liters of air across the microslide for a period of usually ten minutes. The slide is then sealed and sent to the microbiology laboratory for analysis. This type of testing most accurately shows the number and type of airborne mold spores in any specific area.

If you have hired a professional mold remediation contractor to remove the mold from your home, you should demand that third-party post-remediation testing be conducted after the mold remediation process is completed. This testing should be a planned part of the process, and the cost taken into account before the mold remediation begins. (Tests are typically provided and paid for outside of the remediator's scope and cost. This eliminates any conflict of interest in the results.)

Testing the air outside of your home should be performed the same day and time as the air testing inside your home. This also applies to post-remediation testing. This provides an accurate atmospheric picture. An outside mold spore count is similar to the pollen counts you see on the news, which can change substantially from day to day depending on wind, moisture, and other factors. One day the pollen count can be at 3,000, and the next day it can drop to 250.

Theoretically, the air quality inside your home should be better than the outside air. Air conditioning, filters, dehumidifiers, and a plethora of other inside-the-home devices and treatments may help to increase the air quality in your home.

Reading the Microbiology Reports

After mold spore testing is complete, you will receive a report from the laboratory. The report will be organized by the area tested, list the types of mold/fungi that are present, and (if it is a mold spore trap test) show the spore counts of each. First, you will notice the area tested—outside or inside. An outside spore count will be reported first, as it sets the standard for judging the inside air of your home. A typical mold spore count report from a mold spore trap test is shown below.

Test results from the mold spore count for the outside sample show an Ascospore count of 316 and a Cladosporium count of 158.

Sample Location:	Outside		
Report Number:	02ST5051		
Date Analyzed:	11/11/2002		
Time Sampled:	10 Minutes		Debris rating: 2
Flow Rate:	15 Liters/Minute		
Analytical Sensitivity (spores):	23 Spores/m³		
Number of Sweeps:	15		

Sweep Number	1	2	3	4	5	6	7	8	9	10	11	12	13	14	15	Count	Spores/m³
Alternaria																0	0
Ascospore			5							3		2		4		14	316
Aspergillus/Penicillium																0	0
Basidiospore																0	0
Bipolaris																0	0
Botrytis																0	0
Cladosporium		4								3						7	158
Curvularia																0	0
Drechslera/Helminthosporium																0	0
Epicoccum																0	0
Fusarium																0	0
Memnoniella																0	0
Nigrospora																0	0
Pithomyces																0	0
Scopulariopsis																0	0
Stachybotrys																0	0
Stemphyllium																0	0
Ulocladium																0	0
Chaetomium																0	0

In the chart above, the outside mold/fungi levels are reported. Next you will notice a list of types of mold/fungi. The counts of each type of mold found will be reported here.

In this report, Ascospore is noted as being present at a volume rate of 316 spores/m³. Cladosporium is present at a volume rate of 158 spores/m³ with an overall debris rating of 2. This type of test will give you the normal values of your outside atmospheric mold environment, and the standard by which the air inside your home will be judged.

The debris rating is exactly that … a count of the total debris in the air, such as pollen, human skin particles, pet dander, sawdust, dust from sweeping the floor that morning, and many other things. The debris rating tells you if the microbiologist who studied your mold spore sample had a clean "window" to look through. As long as the air sample debris rating is 3 or less, it simply means the overall level of debris in the air did not affect the microbiologist's ability to see the sample clearly, and he or she was able to make an accurate mold spore count. However, when debris ratings climb to 4 or higher, the possibility of achieving an accurate mold spore count diminishes rapidly.

If the counts inside the home are lower than the spore counts outside the home, there is no need for mold remediation in your home. (A small mold problem, such as a moldy shower, should not show up in air testing.) If, however, the inside spore counts exceed the outside spore counts, you have a mold problem and need remediation.

Spore Trap Serial Number:	3920724																
Sample Location:	Inside Condo																
Report Number:	02ST5050																
Date Analyzed:	11/11/2002																
Time Sampled:	10	Minutes					**Debris rating: 1**										
Flow Rate:	15	Liters/Minute															
Analytical Sensitivity (spores):	23	Spores/m³															
Number of Sweeps:	15																
Sweep Number	1	2	3	4	5	6	7	8	9	10	11	12	13	14	15	Count	Spores/m³
Alternaria																0	0
Ascospore		2										2	1			5	13
Aspergillus/Penicillium																0	0
Basidiospore																0	0
Bipolaris																0	0
Botrytis																0	0
Cladosporium																0	0
Curvularia																0	0
Drechslera/Helminthosporium																0	0
Epicoccum																0	0
Fusarium																0	0
Memnoniella																0	0
Nigrospora																0	0
Pithomyces																0	0
Scopulariopsis																0	0
Stachybotrys																0	0
Stemphyllium																0	0
Ulocladium																0	0

The chart above indicates the results from mold spore count testing from the inside of the home. If this is a pre-remediation test, these results indicate that no mold problem exists in the home. You should also receive this same report after mold remediation has been performed. In essence, that report is your mold remediator's scorecard. If this is a post-remediation test, this mold remediator has done an excellent job, and the client's home has received a grade of "pass." Job well done!

Critical Items to Look For

The two most critical components in mold spore count test results are:

- Higher mold spore counts per species of mold inside the home than outside the home
- Different mold spore species present inside the home that are not present in the atmosphere outside the home

In the example given, both Ascospore and Cladosporium were found in the outside atmosphere and inside the home, at lower levels. If different species of mold/fungi were found inside the home and not in the outside environment, it would indicate a mold problem in the home. This is what mold remediators are looking for!

If you need a professional to test for mold, look in your telephone directory under "Mold/Mold Testing" and find a firm with personnel who are certified to perform mold testing. Or go to **www.iaqa.org** and look up a certified firm in your area.

By reading this chapter, you may very well get to know more about mold testing than some of the remediation people who might visit you. This information will give you good ammunition and questions to ask to help qualify your mold testing or remediation specialist. Remember, with mold, accurate knowledge is power. You want the firm you hire to do the job right the first time.

Chapter
5
Mold Cleanup Principles

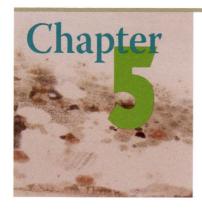

Chapter 5

Mold Cleanup Principles

Goals of Mold Cleanup

Whether the mold infestation is very small and you can clean it up yourself, or it's a larger area requiring professional help, the goals are the same:

- Deal with the source of the moisture that caused the mold.
- Remove the mold itself in a contained way so that the mold spores can't spread to other parts of the room or house.
- Protect the person performing the remediation from exposure.
- Follow up with regular maintenance and inspection to prevent mold from returning.

How Big Is Your Mold Problem?

Consider the size of your mold infestation. If it's very limited and accessible and you're healthy, don't have allergies, and are not a senior or a child, you may be able to handle the job yourself using the proper safety precautions. If it's a bigger area and/or has invaded your heating, ventilating, and air conditioning system, you may consider getting professional help.

Small Jobs

Small infestations involving no more than ten square feet of moldy area are classified as Level I out of five levels designated in some often-quoted mold remediation guidelines developed by the New York City Department of Health & Mental Hygiene. These small mold problems are most often on the surface only of a ceiling or wall, but could also involve shower tiles or other materials. Remember, you must remove the source of the moisture before you attack the mold—or it will just come back again.

This small amount of mold would be a relatively easy job for the homeowner to clean up. A thorough inspection of the area is still a good idea to be certain the mold is not indicative of a larger moisture problem.

If you're planning to clean a small, contained area (where the mold has not infiltrated the wall, subflooring, insulation, etc.), be sure to:

- Use protection—gloves, eye protection, and a NIOSH 95 disposable respirator (from home centers and hardware stores).
- Keep children and the elderly, as well as allergic and immune-compromised individuals, away from the area.
- Seal moldy materials in a plastic bag before carrying them out of your home for disposal.
- Take a direct route to the outside of the house when removing moldy items. If you're working in the basement, for example, exit through the bulkhead door if you have one. If you have to go through hallways, remove any area rugs so that you don't track mold spores on them.
- Clean the area with an EPA-approved fungicide. Leave all cleaned areas to dry throughly.
- Wash moldy clothing or linens in hot water in a washing machine.

Level I—very limited mold problems—usually involve a combination of cleaning (if the materials are hard surfaces such as plastic, metal, glass, and concrete) and removal/replacement (if the materials are porous and absorbent, such as insulation, traditional paper-backed drywall, and carpeting).

Remember, mold can be a serious health hazard. If you have a small mold problem you're thinking of cleaning up yourself, be sure to protect yourself by following all precautions—such as using protective clothing, gloves, an eye mask, and a respirator. To make sure you're taking the right steps, and the job is one you can handle, consult the Environmental Protection Agency's Indoor Air Quality Information Clearinghouse at (800) 438-4318, or contact a professional mold remediator.

Mold is cleaned up when:

- The problem that caused the water intrusion has been fixed—so moisture will not return and start the mold problem again.
- All visible mold and odors have been removed. (There may be staining left behind by mold, but the mold itself should be completely removed.)
- The area has been inspected in the days and weeks after it's been cleaned—to be sure there is no new water intrusion or mold.
- The area can be lived in once again—without any odor or causing any physical sensitivities.

If you're uncertain about your results, call the EPA hotline number in the box on page 42 for advice.

Larger Mold Infestations

Levels II–V of mold remediation involve increasingly larger areas, more precautions, and the

need for professional help. Level II (10–30 square feet) requires careful sealing of all debris and vacuuming with a HEPA filter machine, in addition to Level I precautions. Level III (30–100 square feet) requires that heating/air conditioning grilles be sealed off to prevent the spread of mold spores. Children, the elderly, and anyone with any susceptibility—such as allergies or suppressed immune systems—should be removed from the house during this operation, not just away from the work area.

Level IV (more than 100 square feet) requires still more precautions and professionalism. All remediators should be trained in hazardous materials handling, use of protective equipment, such as full-face respirators and disposable clothing from head to toe, special measures to prevent

contamination of other areas, and monitoring of the air quality in the home. Level V contaminations involve heating, ventilation, and air conditioning systems. Treatment includes not only all the precautions of Levels I-IV, but also professional remediation of ductwork and other HVAC elements with the use of substances that kill microbes.

Mold Caused by Flooding

Water damage from flooding requires quick, usually professional, action. The procedures depend partly on the type of water that has flooded your home. There are three categories of flood water, according to the Institute of Inspection, Cleaning, and Restoration Certification:

1. Clean water from water supply pipes or rainfall
2. "Gray water" from leaking or overflowing appliances (e.g., washing machines, dishwashers) or bath fixtures
3. "Black water" from backed-up sewage or river/pond/lake water that may contain biohazards or chemicals (If left untreated, Category 1 and 2 water will turn to black water in about 5 days.)

The Importance of Quick Action

Flooding that affects carpeting, walls, and furniture/furnishings should be dealt with as soon as possible, by professionals. Growth of bacteria

Mold grows fast at and below the water line in a flood-damaged home.

and mold is extremely likely within 24–48 hours, especially in warm temperatures. If the water level rises above the floor to the wall, mold has an excellent chance of growing behind the wallboard, in which case the moldy materials (wallboard and insulation) should be removed. If any parts of your heating, ventilation, and air conditioning system are flooded, professional cleaning is needed. (See Chapter 9 for more on what to do in case of flooding.)

Steps to Take After a Flood

(adapted from the Centers for Disease Control and Prevention, www.bt.cdc.gov/disasters/floods/cleanupwater.asp)

- Make sure children and pets do not enter the area until the cleanup is completed and any person entering the site is properly protected, wearing:
  - Respirator mask
  - Gloves
  - Goggles
  - Protective clothing if needed
- Discard items that cannot be washed and disinfected. These may include:
  - Carpets and padding
  - Mattresses
  - Furniture
  - Personal belongings such as books and absorbent, non-machine-washable toys
- Discard contaminated building materials, including:
  - Drywall
  - Insulation
  - Wood flooring
- Thoroughly clean all hard surfaces not being removed with hot water and laundry or dish detergent.
- While the area is drying, help the process with fans and dehumidifiers.

It's important to understand the basic principles of mold remediation whether you're planning to clean up a small, very contained patch of mold yourself, or need to hire a professional for a bigger job. Always remember to take precautions, such as covering your skin and using breathing and eye protection.

Chapter

6

Hiring a Mold Remediation Contractor

Chapter 6

Hiring a Mold Remediation Contractor

What do you do if mold has contaminated a substantial area in your home and requires professional treatment? When you begin to look for a mold remediation contractor, how will you determine which firm you can trust to get the job done right at a fair price? Is a cheap solution good enough? Is an expensive one necessarily better? Since mold remediation is a relatively new and unregulated business, trying to answer these questions can be a real headache. If your home has been flooded, you'll also need to take quick action. The bottom line is that you want to find a mold remediator who will be fast, efficient, effective, and fair.

Many contractors have tried to dabble in the mold remediation business only to find that, while they can charge a fair amount of money for it, problems can come up that they're not equipped to solve, and these will be a lot more trouble than a few extra hours of work, the purchase of more equipment, or even a day in court.

Mold is a biohazard and should not be taken lightly. It's a living organism that can dwell in and sicken the human body. Because mold remediation is an action taken to protect your health and that of your family, in addition to your investment in your home, hiring the right company to perform this task is clearly important. After all, you're paying them to eradicate microscopic organisms from your living space. If they do a bad job, you may not see evidence of it until they're pretty far down the road.

Industry Standards

Remember that, unlike asbestos removal, the mold remediation process has not yet been standardized throughout the United States. Some states are working on guidelines and trying to pass measures and laws regulating the practice of microbial (mold) containment and removal. As mentioned in the last chapter, one example is the New York City Department of Health & Mental Hygiene guidelines for mold removal, which include recommended procedures and precautions based on the size of the contamination. Some aspects of this document are based on old asbestos removal guidelines and are still in need of further refinement.

There are several other documents including the EPA Guidelines, IICRC S520 Standards and Reference Guide, and the ACGIH Handbook. The consensus of these documents form a "Standard of Care." You can also check with your state health department for the latest guidelines.

Without national mold removal standards to refer to, the truth is that you need to be cautious. It's been our experience, especially in disaster areas following hurricanes, that many people go into business as mold remediation specialists who were, only 30 days earlier, doing landscaping or another completely different line of work in another part of the country. As with all contractors, check liability insurance, Worker's Compensation insurance, business license registry, and references. If a contractor cannot supply you with *all* of these documents, it may be time to interview someone else. You may also want to check with the Better Business Bureau for any recorded complaints against the company.

Find Out the Basics

It pays to have a basic understanding of what mold is, where it comes from, and how it grows before you start talking to mold remediation contractors. The discussion in Chapter 1 will get you started, and Chapters 2-8 will give you a sense of not only what the health risks are, but the procedures mold remediators commonly use—for testing, removing the mold, and handling your home's contents.

How to Select a Qualified Mold Remediation Contractor

When you have mold in your home, things are bad enough, but if you get taken in by a "bandwagon" mold remediation specialist, your nightmare will only get worse. Start by contacting several mold specialty companies for price estimates. To ensure that the remediation will be handled properly, you also need to ask the right questions:

- *Are you mold-certified?* If not, the conversation need go no further.
- *What organization provided your certification?* Request a copy of their certification. It should be through a national organization in good standing, such as a CMR (Certified Mold Remediator from the Indoor Air Quality Association), or a CMT (Certified Mold

Technician from the Association of Specialists in Cleaning & Restoration). Or the contractor might be a Certified Industrial Hygienist who specializes in mold. A certificate saying "Course Completion" is not a certification, only documentation showing that an individual attended a class. The certification test may never have been taken.

- **Are the individuals who will actually perform the work certified?** If so, ask to see copies of their certifications as well. If the laborers are not certified, be sure to confirm that a certified person will be on site at all times, overseeing the job.

- **How long have you been in business?** You'll want to see evidence of a 2–3 year history of their having been in business under the same name. (Some mold businesses have been sued, closed down, then resurfaced later under a new name.)

- **Can you provide me with at least three references?** Everyone is going to provide you with their best three. Ask them to include a reference for a job where things did not go well. If they have been in this business for any amount of time, they have had a case where everything did not go smoothly. That's just life. What's important is how they handled the problem and made it right with the client.

- **May I have copies of your liability and Worker's Compensation insurance?** Insurance is important. If they get hurt on your property and have no Worker's Compensation or liability insurance, they can sue you for injuries and lost wages.

Negative air machines and plastic sheeting are typically used to keep mold spores from spreading beyond the contaminated area.

- **Do you clean HVAC systems and air ducts?** If not, keep searching. If so, ask how this work is performed. A large, HEPA-rated vacuum device should be connected to your HVAC unit and then to each individual HVAC register in your home. Each register grille should be removed, cleaned, and pressure-vacuumed with high-pressure air hoses that blow all debris into the vacuum device. If they say they spray solutions down the vents and that's all, call the next company.

- **What methods do you use to keep mold spores from spreading?** Typically, flame-retardant plastic sheeting is used to block off other rooms and cover HVAC grilles and other items within the contaminated area. Negative air machines may be used to lower the air pressure within the work area. Another procedure is to have a decontamination area where workers can put on their protective clothing and equipment during the cleanup procedure.

How to Recognize & Avoid Con Artists

Con artists? You bet! The mold remediation industry is full of them. Here are some common ploys:

Scare Tactics

The first sign that you're dealing with a con artist is scare tactics about the health hazards of mold. They often make dramatic statements like:

- "Oh, this is bad!"
- "Oh, this stuff will give you cancer."
- "I'm surprised you're not dead yet!"
- "This stuff is deadly."
- "You better do something because of the children."
- "I've never seen mold like this."
- "It's not good to call a lot of companies about this problem. Word will get out and you'll never be able to sell your house."
- "If you don't do something about this mold, I'll have to report you to the Health Department" … or the EPA, the CDC, your insurance company, the Real Estate Association, your state government, the Department of Agriculture—you name it! Mold remediation contractors have been known to make these outrageous statements. The fact is, there is no agency to report to on mold in your home. (However, if you're a landlord or a restaurant owner, you can be reported to the local health department for mold contamination.)
- "You have toxic mold."
- "You have the bad stuff."
- "You have black mold, and it's always toxic."
- "Whenever you have a water leak, you have mold." (Though water and moisture are good indicators that mold growth could be present, it's not always true. When in doubt, call in a professional to conduct testing.)

Other suspicious statements:

- "When we're finished with your house, it will be mold-free and we'll give you a certificate saying so." (Anyone who tells you your house will be mold-free needs to be shown to your door and not allowed to speak another word. No house is mold-free, nor can it be made mold-free. Mold can only be brought to an acceptable level in your home.)

- "After we remediate the mold, we also do the post-remediation or clearance tests." *Never* use a company that says they will do their own testing before or after any work is done. *Never* use the same company for testing and mold remediation work! This is a clear conflict of interest.

- "We will fog your house and kill all of the mold." (Now what do you do with all the dead mold spores? Just because a mold spore is dead does not mean it is now harmless. Dead mold spores have been known to give off toxic gasses and cause adverse health effects.)

- "All of our chemicals are EPA-approved." (Request the EPA reports called Material Safety Data Sheets, or MSDS, on the chemicals they're using.)

- "It doesn't matter about the water leaks. We can just clean the mold up." (No remediation work should ever be started until all water leaks and humidity problems have been resolved, and the contaminated areas are totally dried out; otherwise, the mold will grow right back.)

- "We need all the money up-front." Most companies require 20%–30% the first day of actual work, when the trucks and equipment are on site and work has started. They receive another 20%–30% when the work is about half-way through, and the remainder after the post-remediation testing has come back "clear."

Electronic Moisture Meters

These are great tools that I use myself to look for and gauge moisture in

Moisture meters are useful for detecting elevated moisture levels, but can be used to deceive—be wary.

various situations. However, be wary of the person behind the meter. These meters have several settings for various materials such as wood, concrete, insulation, drywall, and other materials. Anyone can make the meter alarm go off just by reading the concrete setting on wood surfaces. You don't know what material they have the meter set for, so be skeptical.

Particle Counters

A particle counter is just that … it counts all the particles in the air. Dust, skin flakes, pollen, you name it—if it's in the air, it will show a reading. A con artist can move the particle counter near a vent blowing air, stir up some dust in the room, or use another maneuver to get more particles in the air. Of course, most heating or air conditioning vents have dust in them. Next thing you know, the meter goes crazy and they're screaming "mold!"

Thermal or Moisture Cameras

Thermal imaging has its place in mold exploration. The fact that your home may show moisture on a thermal imaging system doesn't mean there is mold.

"I Have a Special Patented Process for Mold"

While it's true that no one person has cornered the market on good ideas, the fact remains if it's theirs, and it's their patent, and it works, they would be multi-millionaires. The likelihood of them working at your home would be slim to none if they'd invented such a product.

The Test Result Scare

So you think you've found an honest person to work with and have hired this person to conduct testing. He comes in and tests, and now tells you the mold spore counts in your home are astronomically high and that you need thousands of dollars of work performed. This is very common.

Many of these high spore count tests are from tapes or swab samples. Of course these samples will show a very high mold spore count, as they're applied directly to a surface containing mold. This is similar to putting a test thermometer into the flame of your heating furnace while it's running full blast. The results will be a whopping 1,700 degrees, while the living room is at a comfortable 72 degrees. In essence, you may not have a major problem, but the con artist will attempt to scare you with such results.

The Importance of Being Informed

The bottom line is that you have to be informed. Educate yourself, speak to several mold remediation contractors, ask the right questions, use good judgment, and don't let anyone scare or pressure you into anything. Get all the facts and documentation before making any decision.

See Chapter 4 for more information on the various mold spore tests and how they should be used.

For more facts about mold and mold remediation, visit the U.S. Environmental Protection Agency's Web site at: www.epa.gov

Keep in mind, the cheapest firm is probably not the best. Always remember that mold is a biohazard, so you're protecting your family's future health—in addition to your home's value and insurability.

Chapter

7

Insurance Coverage

Chapter 7

Insurance Coverage

If you have a significant mold problem and need a professional remediation contractor, one of the first steps is figuring out who is going to pay for the work. To determine whether your insurance policy will cover any of the expense, you'll need to examine your documentation and understand the terminology and approach of insurance companies in general, and your company and policy in particular.

The insurance term *indemnification* means to put you, your home, your family, and your property back the way it was prior to any sustained loss as covered by and described in your insurance policy. Few policyholders have ever read their insurance policies carefully, and many people have little to no idea what, exactly, they cover.

If you suspect a substantial mold problem in your home, read your insurance policy before contacting your insurance adjuster. A homeowner's policy is actually the size of a small book. Most people only have two or three pages and think that is their policy. Those two or three pages are your declarations, or "dec" pages. These are only summary pages that outline basic and/or major policy coverages, not the detail you'll need to see. If you can't find your entire policy, call the insurance agent who sold it to you and ask for a complete policy copy, including any and all endorsements/amendments since the time of its original issue. They can either e-mail it to you or send you a copy within a few days.

If your home has been flooded, you probably were aware beforehand whether you have flood insurance, and with what company or organization. Homes in a flood plain may be covered by a policy from the National Flood Insurance Program (NFIP), funded by the federal government. While the response can be slow, you will need to take immediate action, getting emergency drying services into your home as

Flood damage can sometimes require a house to be completely gutted.

quickly as possible, then submitting the bill to the insurance company that provides your flood insurance. Some drying companies will submit the bill directly to the insurance company on your behalf.

If floodwater remains in your home for more than 24–48 hours, mold and other damage are extremely likely, in some cases requiring total gutting of the house—walls, insulation, electrical, HVAC system, cabinets, fixtures, flooring, appliances—all of these may have to be replaced.

Being familiar with the details of your policy's coverage just puts you on a level playing field with the insurance company personnel who deal with this every day for a living. With mold growth present in 85% of all cases involving water intrusion (e.g., roof leaks or flooding caused by hurricanes and tornadoes, sink leaks, washing machine overflows, sewer back-ups, water heater leaks, etc.), and with insurance companies' changing policies, penalties, and exclusions, you had better do your homework before you cry "mold."

What Most People Think… and Are Wrong

So, if the mold in my home was caused by a covered loss, such as water intrusion, of course I'm covered! Why would you be afraid that the mold damage would not be a covered loss? The fact is, it should be, but due to new insurance policy provisions and exclusions (resulting in part from recent lawsuits with high-dollar damages), you may have no coverage at all for mold, fungi, bacteria, dry rot, or wet rot.

The odd part about this excluded portion to a covered loss insurance policy provision is that if, for instance, you had a kitchen fire and the flames consumed your kitchen cabinets, while the rest of your home was smoke-damaged, insurance will typically pay not only for the burned cabinets, but also for the repairs needed as a result of the smoke damage. The fire is the direct cause of loss, and the smoke damage is an ancillary damage caused by the fire. This is the same situation as with water and mold—water is the direct cause of the damage, and mold is an ancillary damage caused by the water.

In the case of mold damage, the insurance companies have an altered definition of *damage.* They will readily admit that you had water damage and, if it's covered in your policy, will pay for whatever water damage is visible and documented. But if you have not purchased an additional coverage, or a *mold rider*, you're out of luck for coverage of damage due to mold or fungi.

Why Insurance Companies Limit Mold Coverage

The reason the insurance companies have distanced themselves from mold-related claims hinges on one word—liability. Unlike smoke damage, mold can be a huge health hazard when misdiagnosed, ignored, or left untreated. When the health of infants, children, the elderly, people with allergies or compromised immune systems, and the general public begins to rest on the shoulders of the insurance company's field adjuster—whose experience with mold may be limited—the situation becomes complicated and risky. Negligence and related mold lawsuits are usually not for small dollar amounts; they often range from $250,000 into the millions, depending on what kind of negligence is involved and the amount of the damage caused.

What Happens If I Make a Mold Claim to My Insurance Company?

CLUE Reports

With new information technologies, insurance companies can easily check past claims. Once you make an insurance claim on your home or your automobile, that claim is submitted to the Claims Loss Underwriting Exchange, or CLUE. The purpose of this system is to tip off insurance companies to fraud. CLUE prevents a person from going from one insurance company to another making fraudulent claims—perhaps even the same claim for the same items—and getting paid twice.

The CLUE system bases its information on the policyholder as well as the residence address. So if you submit a mold claim in 2006 with insurance company ABC, and sell your home in 2009, and the buyer has insurance with KYZ insurance company, don't be surprised if you're asked for the post-remediation test results for your past mold remediation claim prior to closing. We were contacted by one of our past clients requesting a "letter of clearance" for the mold work we had performed. They needed it in order to close on the sale of their home because the buyer's insurance company would not insure the home without it. No insurance company wants to pick up liability for anyone's pre-existing damage conditions.

Things to Remember Prior to Making a Mold Claim

Read your insurance policy so that you understand exactly what is covered and what is excluded.

- If you don't understand your policy, call your agent and ask that it be explained to you.
- Simply ask if you have mold coverage. If you have coverage, but the deductible is higher than the cost of the cleanup, just take care of it without involving the insurance company.
- If you have mold coverage, find out what the mold limits are on your policy.
- Confirm what you have been told by your agent by calling the actual insurance company who issued the policy. People make mistakes, and insurance agents are not always perfect. It's your home and your money—check it twice!

Keep in mind that insurance policies generally do not exclude water damage as a whole. They may exclude certain types of water damage, such as groundwater entering your home, even if it's from a broken pipe in the front yard. Other policies may exclude a water loss if action is not taken by the homeowner within 24 hours of the loss to stop damages or stop the leak. Long-term water damage resulting in rot is usually not covered by a homeowner's policy.

If you have too many claims on your homeowner's policy, it could be cancelled, usually once you're past the "honeymoon" period, which typically lasts 12–15 months. If you make a claim during the honeymoon period, the insurer may, in some cases, also choose not to renew your policy at your next renewal date. Generally, after the honeymoon period is over, you can make up to three claims before your policy is cancelled or not renewed. These situations are determined based on the insurance carrier and their loss experience in your area, along with other factors.

What Can Go Wrong with Your Mold Claim?

The answer is, unfortunately, a lot! Everyone wants their home fixed and their damaged possessions replaced. The information you provide to the insurance company adjuster can mean the difference between your claim getting fully paid or completely denied.

Documentation

It's important to identify the leak, flooding, or other water intrusion that caused the mold growth. Since you want to prevent further damage from the presence of water and mold, you'll need to do what you can to dry the area out as much as possible, as quickly as possible.

If possible, after a water event, photograph standing water. If mold appears, these photos will serve as evidence for your insurance claim.

Take pictures that clearly demonstrate the cause (water intrusion) and effect (mold). Take detailed photos of all damage—to the structure and its contents. The photographs will serve as evidence later on of the water event. Give the insurance company copies only ... you need to maintain your own set of originals. Whatever you give to the insurance company to validate your claim becomes their property.

As mentioned earlier, it's also important to get documentation from your professional mold remediation contractor, if you hire one. They can provide you with an assessment of the water intrusion/mold problem as well as a "letter of clearance" verifying that the mold problem has been resolved. This may be needed if you change insurance companies or sell your home.

Public Adjusters/ Appraisal

Should you ever have the need to hire a **public adjuster** (a paid consumer advocate who recovers funds for damages for a policyholder from their own insurance company), give them an opportunity to properly represent you. PAs sometimes recover an amount significantly higher than what an insurance company would be willing to pay at the first settlement offer. They can be helpful in recovering the cost when there are excess damages, such as when complete drywall replacement is needed, and when valuable furnishings are destroyed.

Once again, documentation is key. It is necessary to list water damage separately from mold, bacteria, or dry/wet rot damage so that your situation can be considered for the damages individually and appropriately for removal and/or replacement. Mediation of this type is not binding on either party, and the homeowner can still go to appraisal with the insurance company to get the problem resolved.

Appraisal is a clause in the policy that gives the homeowner remedy to the payment or the estimate of damages assessed by the insurance company if the insured thinks that the insurance company has not accurately evaluated the damages. When demand for appraisal has been correctly submitted, the insurance company usually has 20–21 days to select their appraiser and meet with the homeowner's appraiser on the site in question to try to remedy the situation to all parties' satisfaction.

Know Your Rights

If your mold claim is covered by your insurance company, be aware that the insurance company cannot force you to use a specific contractor. You, as the insured, have the right to hire the contractor of your choice, and it is usually the insurance company's job to negotiate with that contractor.

Insurance coverage for mold remediation differs from state to state. Consult your homeowner's policy and insurance agent for coverage information. Many insurance companies have limited or excluded mold remediation from their policies. You may also want to consult your state commissioner of insurance to confirm your legal rights for insurance coverage.

If you're trying to get coverage on a home, and an insurer denies it because of your previous claims, ask for quotes from other insurers and compare the premiums and what they cover. You can also find out if the state you live in has FAIR (Fair Access to Insurance Requirements) plans. These may be available to owners whose property is thought to be high-risk. Check your credit record too, as insurance companies consider your credit history when you apply for a policy.

Insurance company policies (including the way claims are paid) and the laws that govern them differ from state to state and continually change over time. Following Hurricane Katrina and other natural disasters throughout the U.S., insurance laws are being challenged daily in the courts. What may not have been a covered loss 90 days ago, may be today, and vice versa.

The bottom line is that before you accept the word "no" from your insurance company, read your policy, check with your agent, check with the insurance company home office, and then check with your state department of insurance. In many cases, when an adjuster says not to pay a claim, a little research and a few telephone calls may produce a different answer.

Chapter
8
Your Home's Contents

Chapter 8

Your Home's Contents

Once you know you've got mold in your home, you need to figure out if it's growing on your furniture, clothing, linens, equipment, tools, books, and any other possessions. Mold infestation of these items can be an enormous problem because it can re-contaminate cleaned-up areas or spread to other parts of the house, not to mention increase the overall level of mold hazard in the home.

There's a good chance that the mold you discovered in the basement, attic, or under the sink has found a way to other areas. Now the task begins of finding out how widespread the mold is and exactly where it's growing. A miscalculation in this process can magnify a mold problem and prolong the cleanup process.

What moldy items can you clean and save? What has to be thrown away? Is there any way to salvage irreplaceable and sentimental items or important legal documents? A mold specialist can provide valuable assistance in answering these questions.

It Looks Clean

Many times, to the untrained observer, items look clean when, in fact, mold is there—hiding in shoes, jackets, belts, or boxes and ready to incubate and start the re-contamination process. This can mean that all the money and time you've spent on cleanup has been wasted and you will have to start the remediation process over again.

What If Your Mold Remediator Suggests You Handle the Contents to Save Money?

The red flags should go up! How can professionals doing a professional job allow amateurs to work on their job site? As the homeowner, you do have the right to work on your own property, but how can the mold remediator possibly guarantee your work on their job? This can be a big escape clause for the remediator. Once you handle your own contents, it becomes impossible to tell whether any new mold problems are caused by their poor job of mold remediation or by your re-contamination of the home through incorrect handling of the home's contents.

Cross-Contaminating Your Home

When people discover they have mold in their home, the first thing they want to do is to move all of their contents that look clean from the contaminated area into another part of the house that looks uncontaminated. DON'T DO IT!

Most homeowners are directly responsible for spreading mold from what can be an easily controllable area into their entire home—greatly increasing the cost to fix the problem.

Case in point: Our company received a call that a tree had fallen onto a home and had opened a small hole in the roof. Within days the roof had been repaired, but some rain got in, and there was black mold growing on the bedroom ceiling. We found that the homeowner had done a good job drying out the attic in the damaged area. What they overlooked was the insulation, which had not been dried out correctly and now had visible mold growing on it. The client stated that once the mold appeared, they'd shut off the room from the rest of the house the best they could until we were able to get there, which was the right thing to do.

The client's insurance company requested pre- and post-mold remediation testing by a third party as a part of their requirements. Since the client would soon have a new baby, she requested that the nursery be tested just for safety's sake, although it was not near the damaged bedroom. When the lab results came back, the mold spore count in the baby's room was higher than in the visibly contaminated bedroom. When we examined the nursery, there was nothing but a bed, box spring, mattress, and freshly painted walls—no visible signs of mold, water intrusion, roof damage, or leaks.

This is where experience and detective work come into play. We suspected the client had cleaned the carpet in the nursery with the same steam cleaner she had rented to clean the rug in the mold-contaminated room. Upon questioning her, we found this to be the case. Unknowingly, this client pulled mold from one room, and with the mold-contaminated water, actually seeded the nursery room carpet with mold spores.

Packing Out Your Furniture

Whether or not to pack out your furniture (send your things to storage) and move out of the house can be a difficult decision. On the one hand, you want your home clean, livable, and put back the way it was before the problem. On the other hand, no one likes to be displaced from their home. The main things to consider in making this decision are whether you'll have uninterrupted access during the work process to:

- a full bathroom,
- the kitchen and food supplies,
- sleeping accommodations, and
- heating or air-conditioning.

If the answer is no to any of the above, you may be better off temporarily relocating.

There are several processes that must take place before your home returns to normal:

1. Moving or manipulation of your home's contents
2. Demolition and removal of moldy building materials
3. Mold remediation procedures
4. Post-remediation testing
5. Reconstruction/repairs
6. Final detailed punch list and approval of the finished construction work
7. Moving back into the home and replacing contents where they belong

Depending on the extent of the mold problem and the work required, as well as the contractors you choose, these processes, in their entirety, can take from 30 days up to 1 year.

Items That Tend to Attract Mold

Once moisture is present, wood furniture becomes a welcoming place for mold to grow.

Furniture

Mold is often found on wood and fabric, especially on unfinished wood surfaces, such as the insides of drawers, undersides of tables and upholstered furniture, and bookcases and tables. If the relative humidity in a space is above 48%, mold (often Aspergillus) can grow on all these

materials. Debris that accumulates in upholstered furniture, such as bits of spilled food, soil from shoes and clothing, pet dander, and skin flakes, serve as food for the mold. Mites may take up residence there, too.

Mold can be cleaned from the unfinished backs or undersides of wood furniture with an EPA-approved fungicide. The fungicide should be allowed to dry thoroughly before a finish, such as varnish or shellac, is applied. Always use care to avoid getting varnish or harsh cleaning agents on the finished surfaces of furniture, and get professional advice before you try to clean a valuable piece.

Mattresses & Sofa Cushions

Skin flakes, pollen, and pet dander are just some of the contaminants that can be found in mattresses. Add in a little moisture and you have a

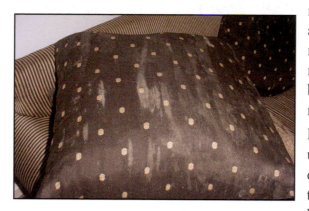

Mold growing on sofa cushions in a contaminated home.

recipe for mold growth and mold-eating mites. Typical mattress materials make an ideal breeding ground for mold.

If mattresses or upholstered sofas or chairs are soaked due to flooding or a major leak, and remain wet for several days, they may have to be thrown away. Mold grows very quickly, and the furniture stuffing is often too thick to be dried out before this happens—even if the piece is removed from the site to a dry location.

Carpet & Area Rugs

Wall-to-Wall Carpet

Wall-to-wall carpet, if left wet for several days, has a good chance of breeding mold. This is why having your home and contents dried out within 24–48 hours is always critical following a water event. The pad underneath the carpet will have to be removed, and the carpet "floated" and dried. This needs to be done by a professional water extraction company. Make sure they use enough drying fans and dehumidifiers. If the water is cleaned up quickly enough, you may be able to save the carpet and only have to replace the pad.

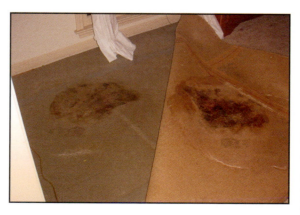

Moldy carpets and pads are often best thrown away.

Carpets that are cleaned should be dried within 24 hours. In many cases, it's best to throw wet carpeting away, carefully cleaning the floor underneath. Mold-contaminated carpet on stairs or in halls should be taken care of promptly because it gets a lot of traffic, which will spread spores throughout the home. Decisions on salvaging carpets and rugs will also be based on what type of water (e.g., Category 1, 2, etc.) they have absorbed. (See "Mold Caused by Flooding" in Chapter 5.)

Area Rugs

These suffer the same effects as wall-to-wall carpet. The good news is that they may be machine-washable or dry-cleanable. It's best to get the water out of them as soon as possible after they become wet. Area rugs should be taken outside to dry prior to cleaning. If this is not possible, contain the rug (in a plastic bag, for example) to keep it from spreading mold spores to the rest of your home. (Get them cleaned as soon as possible. Do not continue to store them in plastic while they're damp.) Valuable Oriental rugs should be cleaned by professionals who specialize in their care. Throw out the old pad and replace it. Rugs that have no great value are probably best thrown out if they've been wet more than two days or have any visible signs of mold.

Curtains & Shades

Curtains and shades are often exposed to mold because they're up against cold windows and condensation. If they're washable or dry-cleanable, you may be able to salvage them. But if they still smell musty or still have stains after cleaning, throw them away.

Clothing & Linens

A very common site for mold is in closets, especially when they're on outside walls that aren't very well insulated. People tend to keep their closet doors shut, so the space inside the closet can be very cold in winter. Since the cold closet sits right next to the heated room, the result is

Mold growing on closet shelves.

condensation, especially in the closet's corners and on the lower walls. This situation is even worse when humidifiers are used in the rooms these closets are in. Condensation may form, starting in the walls on the back paper part of the insulation—and eventually showing up on the interior walls of the closet. Many times mold doesn't appear on the interior walls, but strikes a food source it likes even better, such as leather jackets, belts, shoes, or a purse.

Clothing or linens that have visible mold or smell even slightly musty should be washed in hot water (if the fabric allows) or dry-cleaned. It's even better if you can hang these items out in the sunshine for awhile after cleaning them. If mold spots or odors don't come out in the wash, you'll probably have to throw the items away.

Shoes can usually be cleaned unless they're porous (e.g., suede) with a type of soap that's appropriate for leather. If they're really infested, it's better to throw them out.

Stored Boxes

We highly recommend moving all of the dry items you currently have stored in cardboard boxes to plastic tub containers. This will greatly reduce any chance of water damage or mold now and in the future. Boxes of items are often stored in basements and attics, up against the walls, where leaks can occur. Any cardboard boxes stored in damp and cool areas are susceptible to mold. As mentioned earlier, all moldy boxes should be thrown out.

Good Rules of Thumb

When in doubt … throw it out—better safe than sorry. For the price of saving a single household item, you might jeopardize thousands of dollars of good remediation work.

Some of the Most Commonly Overlooked Items

- Corrugated cardboard boxes. Throw out all moldy boxes. The contents should be properly cleaned, dried, and placed into plastic containers with lids.

- Paper products and fabrics. Throw away all that are in the contaminated area. Important legal documents, family bibles, and irreplaceable photos can be salvaged. First, they must be totally dried out in a contained area. Then they should be HEPA-vacuumed or wiped with a soft cloth using a fungicide (of a type that will not damage the documents). The items can be placed in a small ozone chamber and treated for the appropriate amount of time. These processes should be handled by a professional, such as a restoration specialist.

- Artificial flowers, Christmas decorations (unless they're sentimentally valuable and worth the investment in proper cleaning), indoor living plants in soil, and wallpaper in contaminated areas should be thrown out.

- Carpet, carpet padding, mattresses, and box springs need to be correctly evaluated for contamination. If they're mold-contaminated, trying to save them can be a major pitfall in remediation. Again, consult an experienced mold professional to help you sort out what is salvageable.

Overall, household contents are a very tricky part of mold remediation. This is actually where the majority of mistakes are commonly made. A seemingly safe action like putting one or two items that look clean—but may be harboring mold—into a storage pod may be just the ticket to the re-contamination of an entire home once the stored contents are moved back in.

Chapter 9

What to Expect from Your Mold Remediator

What to Expect from Your Mold Remediator

The Right Steps in the Right Order

When the mold in your home is more than you can safely and effectively remove on your own (based on the guidelines in Chapter 5), you'll need to hire a professional. This chapter will lay out the basic steps in mold remediation and overview the most common technologies/equipment that mold remediation contractors use.

Mold removal is a process, and to be successful, the mold remediator must take certain steps in a certain sequence.

The first step is evaluating the site and developing a plan to correct the problem, as follows:

1. Clearly identify and resolve the source of the water intrusion or humidity problems—before mold remediation is performed.

2. Evaluate the scope of work and develop a program for how the work will be done. This includes considering:

   - What will be done with the home's contents
   - Whether or not the residents will be able to stay in their home while the remediation process is under way
   - How long the process will take
   - Whether there will be post-remediation testing, how long that will take, and who will do it
   - How much, if any, of the home must undergo demolition
   - Who will perform the repairs, and how long that work will take

3. Provide the homeowner with a detailed written estimate explaining what the scope of work will be in each room or area.

The actual mold remediation process will involve the following tasks, performed in this approximate order:

1. Shut down the heating and/or air conditioning system immediately, and keep it shut off throughout the remediation process. Tape off and seal all HVAC registers and returns. Remove, repair, or remedy all water and moisture issues within the structure. If the contaminated area is limited to one or two rooms (or just one separately-controlled story of the house) where there are no air duct returns to suck up mold spores, it may not be necessary to shut down the system. The nearest vents should be checked to make sure they're clean before closing them and taping them off. Remember, when you run the HVAC system, you always run the risk of cross-contamination. As you tear out contaminated walls, ceilings, carpet, and pads, you're stirring up a lot of dust and spores. Even though the negative air machines and other equipment will be up and running, and containment measures are set up, it's best to minimize any risk.

2. Set up dehumidification units and run them until the day the job is over and post-remediation testing has been scheduled.

3. Clean and then store in a clean, dry space all furniture and furnishings from the affected area. (Otherwise, any mold on the contents will continue to grow in the storage area and can re-contaminate the home.)

4. Set up proper containment area(s). Containment basically means keeping a contaminated area to and within itself, thereby preventing the spread of mold—by traffic or air circulation—to other areas of the home. At the start of the project, your mold remediator

Proper containment and the use of negative air machines are important steps in preventing cross-contamination during remediation.

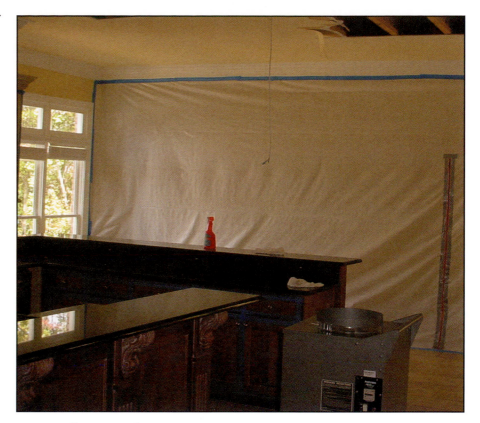

will set up a decontamination chamber where workers will store and clean their contaminated suits and equipment.

5. Use negative air machines in the contained areas to achieve negative pressurization.

6. Set up HEPA-filtered air scrubbers.

7. Selectively demolish and remove debris in designated areas.

8. Remove the mold by the method appropriate to the situation.

9. Clean the heating and air conditioning units and all ductwork with HEPA-rated equipment. Replace filters and insulation and, if necessary, some types of ductwork. (If the plenum is made of duct board, it will have to be removed and replaced. Flex duct is cheaper to remove and replace than to clean in most cases, and metal plenums and ductwork can almost always be cleaned. If furnace or air conditioning system elements have been flooded, they will need to be replaced.)

10. Vacuum all surfaces with HEPA-filtered vacuuming systems.

11. Wipe down every square inch of surface by hand with an EPA-approved biocide, preferably with an antibacterial, antifungal, and antiviral cleaning solution.

12. Allow the air scrubbers to run (typically for 24–48 hours) after the remediation process has been finished.

13. Perform post-remediation testing to ensure that mold spore counts are at an acceptable level. This should be done by a certified mold testing/inspection company, separate from the contractor performing the remediation. (No one should enter the structure without protective gear until the post-remediation test results are back and are satisfactory.)

14. If the post-remediation verification test results are unacceptable, the remediation process should be redone and the area tested again until the results are satisfactory. (An unsuccessful test can mean your mold remediator did not do the job right the first time… or it might mean that there is a "hidden reservoir" of mold that requires additional work. If there is legitimately more work needed, the remediator should show the client the additional contaminated area. If a remediator says there is a lot more work than they first thought, put on your respirator, gloves, and mold suit and go look for yourself. Also, be sure to get, in writing, a statement that if the post-test fails, the remediators must re-clean the area free of charge until it passes.)

The process just outlined gives an idea of standard mold remediation methods that are widely used and accepted. Depending on your situation, your contractor may recommend another type of specialty remediation treatment, such as fogging, blasting, or encapsulants (explained later in this chapter).

What to Expect During the Remediation Process

It's helpful to know, up front, what the mold remediation process involves. Most people are upset when they find that they have to leave their homes for a few weeks while the work is done. Some choose to shortcut the work so they can stay in their homes or return to them quickly. It's important to ask the following questions and get a good understanding at the start:

- **How long will this process take?** The answer depends on how much work is going to be done and how many people will be working on your project. Mold remediation is labor-intensive. A small remediation company may not have enough manpower to do your job as quickly as you'd like. To give you an idea of how long remediation work takes, a 2,000-square-foot house might, on average, take between 10–13 days—if remediation includes the processes described earlier in this chapter, including removal of all drywall, flooring, and appliances—basically taking the house down to the studs.

- **What testing will be done after remediation is complete?** Post-testing should immediately follow the remediation process. Laboratory results can be overnight-mailed, and same-day results can typically be obtained via e-mail.

• **How much should mold remediation cost?** This is a tough question. You're paying not only for the equipment, materials, transportation, crew (including their benefits, etc.), and the company's overhead, but also for what your remediator knows and has been trained to do—how to get the job done right the first time. Mold remediation charges can vary widely between contractors for the same work. We suggest you get a few bids. (See Appendix C for more on remediation costs.)

Flooding

In the case of a major flood that affects a widespread area, such as New Orleans and other Gulf Coast areas after Hurricane Katrina, the only immediate action you may be able to take is what you and your family can do yourselves. All the contractors in the area will tend to be working on their own homes or their families' and friends' first. If your house is the only one or one of just a few flooded in the area, you should be able to get an emergency water extraction company quickly—and *time is of the essence.* Then work on getting bids to repair your home. In areas of widespread flooding, homeowners may have to wait 1–6 weeks for an insurance adjuster to be able to get to their homes to assess the damage.

If your home is affected by a major flood, here are some things you can do to minimize your damages while you wait for a professional.

- Get all the water (or mud/water) out as soon as possible.
- Remove the carpet and carpet padding in the flooded areas.
- Remove all tackless carpet strips.
- Remove baseboards that were exposed to direct water damage.
- Remove all flood-damaged drywall.
- Remove all flooded cabinets, fixtures, and appliances.
- Place dehumidification and drying units in the structure until it is dried out.

You can use a shop vac, a pump-out unit, shovels, buckets, etc. to get water and mud out of your home. But keep in mind that when a home floods, the power for an electric pump is cut off because of the fire hazard and risk of electric shock. If the flood area is substantial and many homes are damaged, portable electric generators are few and far between. Note: due to the dangers of using electricity in and around water, always exercise extreme caution when working in flooding situations.

Remember: prior to removing anything from your home, photograph, photograph, photograph! You can't have too many pictures documenting your damages.

Interview the remediators as to their knowledge of mold and the remediation processes they use. Ask for their proof of insurance (Worker's Compensation, general liability), proof of certifications in mold removal, a current business license, and references. If a general contractor is doing the work, keep in mind that mold and pollution coverage are typically not included in a contractor's general liability policy. Look for "pollution" coverage at additional premium expense. (See Chapter 6 for more on hiring a mold remediation contractor, the Resources for organizations that certify mold remediators, and Appendix C for some national average remediation costs.) Common sense is the best tool you can use when selecting a mold specialist.

Repairing Your Home

One of the best things you can do to get back into your home fast is hire a general contractor who is also an experienced and certified mold remediator. This type of company can schedule the reconstruction of your

Mold remediation can leave your home in need of repair and rebuilding. Hiring your contractor to begin work immediately after remediation is complete will limit the time the contaminated space is unlivable.

home back-to-back with the remediation work. If this combination service is not available, arrange a meeting between your general contractor and your mold remediator as soon as you've selected the remediation company. They can do a walk-through of your property together, clarifying what the remediation work will involve, and the scope of work each of them will be responsible for. The contractor can then work up an estimate for the repairs he will perform, along with a timetable for when they can get you back into your home.

Common Remediation Methods

Hand Sanding & Wire Brushing

The traditional method for cleaning/removing mold is manually scraping and sanding the material (usually wood). This approach is labor-intensive, since every stud, joist, electrical wire, box, and outlet—virtually every surface—must be cleaned—first be HEPA-vacuuming and then by sanding (for wood) or wiping down with a bio-wash solution.

The next step is vacuuming and removing the debris, then applying a biocide chemical to kill remaining mold spores, and finally applying an antimicrobial coating.

Sandblasting

The basic idea behind this method is sound, but its flaws have outdated it. Since mold only grows into any object to a depth of two microns (about the thickness of two human hairs), sandblasting is overkill. Whether it's on the surface of painted drywall or on the inside of the wall under the insulation, sandblasting can seriously damage the surface and even weaken structural lumber.

Another problem with sandblasting is that sand is heavy and dirty, and may itself contain mold. It does not have any mold-killing qualities, and it holds moisture. If it's not removed from the job site correctly, it may actually enhance mold growth. Removing heavy sand from spaces with low ceilings, such as attics and crawlspaces, and around water and electrical lines, can be very difficult.

Dry Ice Blasting

The drawbacks of dry ice blasting are, if used incorrectly, possible damage to the structure and the risk of airborne mold being spread. It can also be an expensive, slow process, as it requires a more costly material (dry ice pellets) and additional equipment.

Utilized correctly, however, dry ice blasting can be an effective mold removal method. Remember, it does not kill mold—blasting generally only removes the mold from the contaminated surfaces. Containing it and getting it out of the home are crucial steps your mold remediator must address.

Soda Blasting

Soda blasting is similiar to sandblasting, but uses baking soda and a lower pressure. It's a dry process that dislodges mold, dirt, and bacteria from materials, such as structural framing members, without damaging the wood. (It's also used to remove paint, graffiti, soot, and grease from masonry, metal, and plastic materials.) Soda blasting has the added advantage of eliminating odors. After the mold has been removed and vacuumed, an antimicrobial agent is usually sprayed on the surface to prevent mold from re-growing in the future.

Soda blasting uses compressed air and special equipment to deliver a fine mist of baking soda, a nontoxic material that doesn't harm humans or the environment. Like dry ice blasting, soda blasting produces debris (mold and wood residue) that must be removed by the remediation contractor.

Foggers

The term "fogging" has been loosely used throughout the mold remediation industry. Usually, fogging is the cheapest form of mold remediation available, basically because it doesn't involve much labor. The contractor places the machines in your home, leaves and lets them run for a period of time, then comes back and picks up the equipment, and you get a bill.

This sounds very appealing to many people, because they only have to leave their house for a day or two. No one is tearing out any walls or ceilings, and they don't have to wait for anyone to replace drywall, insulation, flooring, carpet, or paint. You may even get some kind of guarantee. Life couldn't be better! Actually, if you, your children, spouse, or pets are not sensitive to mold, this might work for you—for how long, however, no one knows.

Companies that use foggers often state that the chemicals they use are approved by the Environmental Protection Agency (EPA), and that the fog will kill all of the mold, leaving the home mold-free. But that still leaves questions. If you kill mold spores, shouldn't you clean up the dead spores? When a mold spore dies, does it emit harmful or toxic gases through its process of decay and deterioration? The answer is "yes," and if you or your family members are mold-sensitive, the gases produced by decaying mold spores may cause adverse health effects. In the old days, poisoning rats was an acceptable practice until they died behind the walls and smelled for months. The same is true with decaying mold spores.

And, of course, no home is mold-free. Ideally, mold will have been brought down to an acceptable level after remediation.

Any company that uses foggers should be able to provide a list of the chemicals they use, a copy of the EPA labels for those chemicals, and a protocol of how they apply them.

Ozone

Ozone is a type of fogging. It's a natural product of our environment—Earth is surrounded by a natural ozone layer. Ozone is also a unique tool in the world of mold remediation. Since it's a deadly gas in concentrated form, ozone should be used only by authorized professionals. In fact, the EPA discourages its use in remediation. (Many companies sell low-level ozone generators for household use and air purification, though the quality of these appliances varies widely.) So what is good, and what is bad about ozone?

In the mold remediation process, ozone chambers have been used to rescue important legal documents, photos, family bibles, artwork, and other treasures that were contaminated and would have been lost to mold. Other situations that favor the use of gas and/or fogging equipment, such as ozone generators, are tight spaces where there is physically no room for a human being to enter and work in the contaminated space. Ozone and ozone generators should be treated with great caution. They are not an all-purpose solution for the total remediation of mold in every environment, but with correct supervision, ozone does have its applications.

Sprayers

Some remediators claim that they can treat your entire home and its contents by spraying them with one or more chemicals. These will also be among the lowest cost estimates you receive for mold remediation. Spraying *sounds* like a good solution—you may not have to move out of your home, or if you do, it will only be for a day or two. Similar to fogging, this method doesn't disturb your home's contents. And there's no demolition and rebuilding.

This technique can be effective if you have a building that is completely gutted down to the studs and all your furniture is moved out. Spraying EPA-approved solutions may not be a bad idea if it is backed up by other mold removal techniques.

One thing to be wary of is companies that tell you they can completely clean all your HVAC systems and ductwork too, just by spraying. The fact is, mold remediation for HVAC systems and air ducts should be done with HEPA-filter-rated equipment.

Do-It-Yourself Mold Remediation

There are many jobs that the weekend warrior may want to take on, but when it comes to a major mold infestation, you might want to think twice. The problem is that if you miss even a small amount of spores, the chances are very high the mold will return.

Common problems amateur mold remediators face:
- Not knowing what to keep and what to throw away
- Not knowing what cleaning solutions work best, and thinking that bleach will kill the mold
- Not having the special equipment to do the job
- Not knowing how to set up containment—and inadvertently spreading the mold to other parts of the structure
- Not knowing how to clean the HVAC system properly
- Not having the protective equipment to keep from getting sick while doing the work

The fact of the matter is that one-third of all the mold jobs we've been called to do are situations where remediation has already been performed by someone else, but the job was done poorly, and the mold came right back. The homeowners have already borne the hardship of being displaced from their home once and spent all their insurance (or a good deal of their own) money. Usually we are called in after all the walls have been replaced and painted, with new carpet already in place. It often all has to come out, and the homeowner has the inconvenience of moving out again, not to mention the additional expense.

Bleach & Mold

"Just throw some bleach on it, and the mold will be gone." This is one of the biggest pieces of misinformation out there about mold. If it were that

A contractor at this condominium bleached the walls and then repainted. The mold grew back in 60 days because the bleach did not kill the mold on the framing inside the walls.

simple, there would be no mold remediators. Certain types of mold are chlorine-resistant. People apply bleach, but the mold comes right back. In fact, it never went away.

Many contractors who have been involved in lawsuits used bleach or even swimming pool treatment chemicals to try to eradicate the mold. They learned the hard way that there are no shortcuts to doing the job right.

When it comes to professional mold remediation, fancy equipment alone is not enough. Sprayers, foggers, blasters, thermal cameras, and more—all of it is worthless unless the people operating the equipment are properly trained and experienced and have knowledgeable, experienced supervision.

Chapter 10

Mold-Resistant Construction Methods & Materials

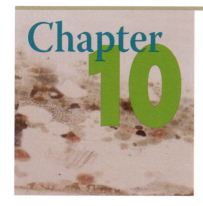

Mold-Resistant Construction Methods & Materials

Mold-Preventing Construction Methods— Basic Principles

While mold is everywhere, we can keep it at bay through good maintenance and the right approach to home construction. This chapter will explain ways in which you can build or remodel a home with mold prevention in mind. Chapter 11 follows with guidelines on important maintenance practices.

If you're building a new home or remodeling an existing one, one of the objects, in terms of mold-prevention, is to have a low permeability rating—or minimal chance of unwanted moisture entering the home. Here are some tips.

Foundations, Basements, & Crawlspaces

For a new home or addition, select a **building lot** with a high enough water table and away from underground springs. Determine **drainage** with a percolation test, normally required to obtain a building permit. The **slope** of the land is a key factor (to avoid water running toward the house).

Waterproof and seal **foundation walls** per building code requirements, and insulate them to minimize condensation caused by the temperature difference between the earth and the home's interior. A concrete sealer can also help prevent moisture from seeping into a basement or crawlspace.

Positive slope allows water to drain away from the foundation.

Being open to the outdoors, **crawlspaces** tend to be damp—so they're a challenge in terms of keeping mold out. If it does become established there, mold can migrate through any openings in the floor to the house above. (In fact, some mold specialists recommend not having ventilated crawlspaces at all in regions with high humidity.) Nevertheless, there are some preventive measures you can take:

- Use a dehumidifier and mildewcides.
- Install a heavy-duty plastic vapor barrier (8 mil or thicker) on the ground.
- Regularly inspect for—and clean up—mold.

If you have an **unfinished basement**, first make sure the dirt is absolutely dry. Then use a heavy-duty plastic vapor barrier, and make sure there are no holes in it. (Don't use regular plastic sheeting, which is more likely to be damaged during installation or over time.) A concrete floor is a better solution, and it should also have a vapor barrier underneath. Waterproofing compound can be mixed into the concrete to make the floor more resistant to water intrusion.

In basements older than 40 years or so, there probably is no plastic sheeting beneath the concrete floor. In this case, clean and then paint the floor with a special concrete paint designed for indoor use.

Make sure **concrete floors** and walls are thoroughly dry before installing wood flooring. (See "Material Handling" later in this chapter for more on measuring moisture content in concrete.)

It's usually best to avoid carpeting in **finished basements**. Use ceramic or resilient tile, stone, or even hardwood flooring, with throw rugs that can be washed frequently. If hardwood flooring is to be installed over concrete, wood sleepers should be installed first, over the moisture barrier, to keep the finished wood from coming into contact with the concrete.

Provide a dehumidifier and air conditioning for the space. Use foil-coated sheet foam insulation, where building codes allow, instead of rolled fiberglass behind drywall in basement walls. Also avoid built-in wood shelves or storage units. Wood supports mold growth; metal or plastic—*if kept clean and dust-free*—are less likely to harbor mold.

Framing & Insulating

Use durable species or preservative-treated woods as required by building codes for certain framing applications. Treat dry lumber with a spray-on fungicide. Use sheet, roll, or batt insulation instead of blown-in types. Consider encapsulants and new mold-resistant insulation products.

Roofs & Drainage

New homes should be sited such that the sun can evaporate any dampness that has accumulated on the structure overnight. The roof—new or repair/replacement—should have **overhangs** to help carry roof drainage farther away from the structure itself and from all doors and windows. Roofs have a lot of surface area and channel a lot of water. A **steeper pitch** allows water and snow to slide off quickly so it has less opportunity to leak through.

Make sure **shingles** are nailed to a proper depth. In hurricane areas, hand-nailing and tabbing or cementing them may be preferable to mechanical stapling. **Tile roofs** require certain types of underlayment and "waterlocks"—pieces (ribs and channels) that help prevent water from migrating under the tile. Fastener holes are another factor in water migration.

Flashing is a thin sheet of material, typically metal, that is used to prevent water penetration or to direct the flow of water. Flashing is used especially at roof hips and valleys, for penetrations (like chimneys and vent pipes), and where a roof joins a vertical wall. Improper flashing is a common cause of roof leaks, either because it was installed incorrectly or has become bent and worn over time. **Valleys** (between roof angles) have to be constructed properly (e.g., wider at the bottom than the top) to prevent debris from getting trapped and holding moisture. Shingles at the eaves should project beyond the edge of the roof framing.

Roof overhangs and properly installed gutters will allow water to drain away from the structure and prevent moisture from penetrating the walls and roof.

Make sure all rain **gutters and downspouts** are properly installed and sized correctly for your roof. If rain gutters are too small to handle the amount of water coming off your roof, or downspouts don't carry all the water far enough away from the structure, you could have pooling at the foundation and leaks into your home. Even inexpensive splash blocks can make a big difference in redirecting water from downspouts.

Siding

Wood siding should be back-primed before it's installed, and it should stop well above the ground. If it's too close, the wood will stain and rot, which can lead to mold in the sheathing below.

EIFS (sometimes referred to as "stucco" or "fake stucco") siding should be durable and keep moisture out, provided it's installed correctly by a contractor certified by the system manufacturer. (For more information, contact the EIFS Industry Members Association at **www.eima.com**)

New, high-performance materials are available for moisture barriers for this type of siding. They allow moist air to flow out of the structure, so it does not become trapped in the wall cavity and cause mold. There are many specific requirements for EIFS installation that must be followed to prevent moisture problems.

Windows, Skylights, & Doors

One of the biggest causes of damage to homes is water leaking at doors and windows. Some ways to prevent this include:

- Choosing the right window for the climate and selecting insulated windows to prevent condensation.
- Using flexible, rubberized, self-adhesive flashing.
- Applying high-grade flexible sealant at corners of aluminum window frame assemblies.
- Making sure windows are installed right-side-up so the weepholes can drain properly.
- Making sure the water seal isn't broken after painting when workers clean up with a razor-type scraper.
- Installing window and door flashing correctly—away from and over joints. If it's not done right, flashing can actually direct water into the walls.
- Placing and properly lapping air infiltration barriers before new windows, exterior doors, and trim are installed. This ensures that the vertical joints between the exterior window casing (or trim) and the sheathing are sealed. Otherwise, moisture may be driven into the sheathing.
- Painting the top and bottom surfaces of doors, as well as finishing the other four sides.
- Using the right finish for the situation. For example, a clear finish will not stand up well to extended weather exposure.

Heating, Ventilating, & Air Conditioning

"Tighter" houses, with less ventilation, have been built since the energy crisis in the 1970s. While they conserve energy by keeping conditioned air in, and outside air out, they also keep moisture from evaporating, leading to mold and mildew. To minimize ventilation problems, here are some things you can do:

- Make sure you have appropriate vents in your roof.
- Use fans in the kitchen and baths to exhaust moist air. Choose the right size of exhaust fan to do the job.

Properly vented range hood.

- Vent combustible appliances, such as furnaces, water heaters, and fireplaces, since they, too, produce water vapor. Make sure these appliances have air circulation by keeping doors open to the rooms they're in and ensuring their vents are properly connected, have no holes or cracks, and are not blocked.
- Route dryer vents to the outside, and keep them lint-free.
- Use metal ductwork—preferably without insulation.
- Insulate ductwork (on the outside of the duct) that goes through an unconditioned area like an attic, basement, or crawlspace. Seal duct joints, then apply spray foam or flexible insulation around metal supply ducts, trunks, and plenums. (Flexible ductwork should not be used in crawlspaces, as vermin can gain access to the house through them.)
- Make sure drip pans for cooling coils are draining properly.
- Avoid central humidification systems. If you do use them, use the type that has water flowing through with a pump, versus a reservoir that holds water.
- If you use an air purifier to help reduce contaminants, including mold, consider a unit that offers more than one technology, such as HEPA filters and ionizers.
- Consider installing radiant floor heating in a new home. Not only is it comfortable and efficient, but it helps dry up floor spills.

Plumbing

Being a water source, plumbing is clearly one of the most important items in mold prevention. Here are some suggestions:
- Avoid having plumbing supply lines in exterior walls to minimize condensation. If pipes must be run in exterior walls, insulate between the pipe and the sheathing, not between the pipe and the home's interior … since you want to keep it a similar temperature to the conditioned air inside.

- If cold water pipes pass through unconditioned spaces, insulate them with ½" insulation or the equivalent to avoid condensation. This applies to piping in outside walls in warm climates and in crawlspaces during the summer in colder climates.
- Don't install plumbing supply pipes in concrete floors or slabs, because they'll be more likely to deteriorate and leak over the years.
- Pressure-test pipes before they're covered up by finished walls to see if there are any leaks.
- In new home construction, try to group plumbing lines and sewer drain lines, and provide easily accessed panels so pipes can be checked, maintained, and repaired in the future.

Walls & Floors

Since the paper covering on **drywall** allows for mold growth, consider paperless drywall for new construction. (See "Mold-Resistant Construction Materials" later in this chapter.) Drywall behind moist environments such as ceramic tile in bathrooms, especially showers, should be specially rated for moisture resistance and primed at all ends with waterproof mastic. Standards must also be followed for installation of tile mortar, expansion joints, grout, and sealers.

Closets on under-insulated outside walls are notorious for mold growth. In the winter, the cold walls meet the heated air inside, causing condensation … and eventually mold on the clothing or other items stored there, and sometimes on the closet walls and floor. In new homes, exterior walls around closets should be well-insulated, and the space should have adequate heat. In an existing house with a poorly insulated exterior wall along the closet, you might switch solid doors for louvered ones that allow ventilation … or leave the closet doors open.

As mentioned previously, moist **carpet** is a perfect environment for mold growth. Don't use carpeting in bathrooms, laundry rooms, mudrooms or other entry areas, and sunroom/porches that are often open to the outdoors. Carefully consider whether to use carpet for finished basements.

Slope the floor in a new **laundry room** to a drain, in case of a washing machine overflow.

Landscaping

Irrigation or sprinkler systems can cause problems if they're directed toward the foundation. Make sure **shrub beds** and planting areas next to a structure drain properly, away from the house. Don't plant shrubs too

This sprinkler is too close to the home's foundation, and may cause water damage that could lead to mold growth.

close to the house, and select the appropriate size plants for your home. Consult the nursery where you purchased them—or look in a good plant book—to find out how large your shrubs will grow over time, so they won't trap moisture up against the house.

Don't allow organic materials, such as wood chips, to come in contact with wood siding or trim. Install **stone or tiles as a buffer** between damp earth and the foundation. If necessary, have **French drains, drainpipes, or culverts** installed to direct water away from your home.

The first part of this chapter dealt with design and construction methods to prevent mold. This next section will address another important factor—the products and materials that are installed in a home, and how to handle them on the site to prevent mold problems later.

Proper Handling of Construction Materials to Prevent Mold

Wet lumber that is not properly dried before installation risks growing mold later, causing contamination that can go unnoticed for a long time beneath the drywall.

Lumber

Lumber should be scheduled for delivery close to when it will be used. The builder should inspect it for mold when it arrives and reject any that

does have it. If lumber must be stored outside, it should not be in direct contact with the ground, to prevent it from absorbing moisture and to provide for air circulation. Lumber can be temporarily covered with plastic sheeting or, even better, house wrap, which will let water vapor vent out while keeping rainwater off the wood. The roof and side walls of a house under construction should also be covered to protect exposed wood from rain before the final roofing, siding, doors, and windows are installed.

Interior Materials

Materials that will be installed on the inside, such as drywall, interior doors, flooring, cabinets, and trim, should be scheduled for delivery after the home's exterior has been sealed, and with enough time allowed for these materials to acclimate to conditions in the house before they're installed. If these materials must be briefly stored outdoors, cover them with plastic sheeting or tarps and keep them off the ground.

Use of Drying Equipment

Equipment should be available, as needed, to speed drying time for materials like concrete, plaster, and paint. Fans, dehumidifiers, and portable heaters are sometimes used, depending on the site conditions and temperature.

A moisture meter can be used to measure the degree of moisture in wood to ensure that wood framing and sub-flooring, for example, are adequately dry (about 12%–14% moisture content) before finish materials are installed. A calcium chloride test can determine whether a concrete slab is dry enough before installing wood flooring. (The National Wood Flooring Association recommends that wood flooring not be installed over concrete if the moisture readings are more than 7 lbs using the calcium chloride test.)

Inspections & Mold Tests During Construction

Builders should check all installations that involve penetrations to the outdoors, such as vapor barriers and doors, windows, roof vents and pipes, and deck installations, to make sure there are no leaks. Some builders also test for mold—during the construction and when the project is completed.

Another important step is removal of all construction wood debris and concrete forms from the site. These materials can be a source of mold infestation that can spread to the house.

Fortunately, professional organizations like the Associated General Contractors and the National Association of Home Builders have created guidelines for their members to help them take the right steps to avoid mold in construction. Not only does this make for happier customers, but it helps contractors avoid lawsuits, insurance problems, and the expense of redoing their work.

Mold-Resistant Construction Materials

Over the past few decades, many construction materials have changed. They reduced the time and cost of constructing a home, but they also changed our environment and made our homes more susceptible to mold. What used to be plaster is now gypsum wallboard or "drywall"—with a paper backing that allows mold to grow. What used to be solid wood is now chipboard—with fiber and glue that provide a breeding ground and food for mold. Unfortunately, some of the new ecologically friendly materials like bamboo and cork are also susceptible to mold, since they're porous and can retain water.

The building industry has realized that mold has become a serious issue and has started producing full lines of mold-resistant products. Some of them, like paperless drywall, resist mold by avoiding use of materials that support mold growth. Others use chemical processes, such as Microban®, which kill microbes. Microban is an ingredient in carpet, paint, caulk, and grout, to name just a few mold-resistant construction products.

The next time you build a home or have repair or remodeling work done, you may want to consider some of these. While there is no "silver bullet" to make sure mold won't grow on a surface, these materials and products are worth investigating as a big step toward minimizing mold damage.

Paperless Drywall

Mold loves drywall. As you have seen illustrated in this book, its paper covering is a favorite food source. Many homes have to be completely gutted and have all the drywall removed due to mold contamination. Even aside from the mold threat, once drywall has been wet, it usually loses its integrity. It's like a sponge—when it comes in direct contact with water, it soaks it up through capillary action. Water-damaged drywall usually splits at the seams and needs to be replaced.

The new paperless drywall gives homeowners a big advantage in the war against mold. In most of the mold-contaminated homes we've worked on, water intrusion starts at one location in the home, where the mold spores germinate, grow, and begin to release new spores. Then the mold spreads from room to room. Since, in most homes, drywall makes up 70%–80% of the total surface area, there's a good chance the mold will start on, and spread to, this material.

The drywall you have now is most likely paper-sheathed, and mold and termites both eat paper. In theory, paperless drywall could save approximately 70%–90% of the drywall demolition in a mold-contaminated home, providing the water intrusion and water damage were isolated to a particular area. Where there is no moisture or food source, the mold spores would go dormant and not cause any further problem as long as the house remains dry.

Paperless drywall is being manufactured by several of the major drywall manufacturers, such as Georgia Pacific, National Gypsum, and USG. It's made of a gypsum core sheathed in fiberglass or vinyl instead of cellulose, so mold and termites won't eat it. It comes in standard-size drywall sheets, 4' x 8' or 4' x 12', though it's a bit heavier. It is stocked at major home

Paperless drywall looks just like traditional paper-backed drywall, but resists mold growth.

centers and building supply distributors and is more expensive than regular drywall. (As of this book's printing, a 4' x 8' sheet of half-inch paperless drywall costs around $11, while the same-size standard drywall is around $8.)

The product is hung, taped, and floated, and can be textured and painted like any other drywall. Again, it's not *mold-proof,* since mold can grow on virtually any surface under the right conditions, but it is mold-resistant, since it offers no food source for mold. The big advantage is that you have an inorganic surface inside the wall facing the studs, and mold cannot feed on it. However, since the studs in most homes are still made of wood, and mold will feed on wood, you might consider having your studs for a new home sprayed with a coating of mold-resistant encapsulant.

A Word of Warning

Some people are allergic to certain pesticides and can have some of the same health problems with these as are caused by mold. Care should be taken in using products with mildewcides or pesticides in the homes of people with chemical sensitivities.

Mold-Resistant Paints

After you've installed your paperless drywall, you may want to take another step to make it even more difficult for mold to grow. Mold-resistant paint started when manufacturers added what they referred to as a mildewstat, or mildewcide, to their paints. Since, in most cases, the anti-mold chemical was under 2% of the total volume of paint in the container, it was not listed as an ingredient. Once mold began to become such a big issue, some paint manufacturers started to advertise that their paint was mold-resistant. Then the Environmental Protection Agency started to classify paints with mildewcides as pesticides requiring EPA approval.

Paint as a Cause of Poor Indoor Air Quality

We were called to a home where a child had been ill with respiratory problems and fatigue. When she was away from the home for a day, she felt normal. Her mother had the house tested for mold, but laboratory results were negative. We asked what had changed in the home over the last six months and found that new hardwood floors had been installed and the interior of the home had been painted.

We employed a Certified Industrial Hygienist, who tested the new flooring (pressed, pre-manufactured, and finished flooring) and the paint. He found that the paint contained a mildewcide that could be causing the girl's sensitivity. The girl's mother took her to an allergist, who found that she was, indeed, sensitive to that compound. The walls were scraped and repainted with a regular paint, and the child recovered.

All mold-prevention measures have their place and applications. It's best to become educated about what materials you're putting into your home, because taking them out might be just as—or even more—expensive than it was to have the work done initially.

Encapsulants

Encapsulation is a very useful tool in the world of mold remediation, but it shouldn't be viewed as a quick and total cure. Like paints, encapsulants lose their integrity over time, which is why the manufacturers' guarantees tend to be for two to five years, provided the paints are applied according to the manufacturers' application specifications.

Also, some mold remediators will tell you it's not necessary to remove the mold contamination; just spray the encapsulant over the mold, and it will kill it and seal it up. This type of proposal usually comes with the low bid (or it should). The proper way to use an encapsulant is to first remove the moisture source (leaking pipe or roof, condensation, etc.) and then perform the mold remediation work. The last step should be applying the encapsulant.

Encapsulants are great for areas such as crawlspaces and attics, where there are no environmental controls (heating or air conditioning). It's also a good idea, though expensive, to encapsulate almost any area after a remediation process has been completed. It's just another measure to reduce your risk of mold re-growth.

Insulation

Some insulation manufacturers have developed products that contain a borate-based fungicide to prevent mold. These products must be tested in order to be registered by the Environmental Protection Agency to ensure that the fungicide will, in fact, resist mold growth when exposed to mold-favorable conditions. Some of these products are also flame-retardant and claim to absorb any moisture that enters the wall and redistribute it, allowing a wall to dry in a "controlled" manner.

Other Mold-Resistant Products

A wide variety of construction product manufacturers offer a mold-resistant version of their product—from house wrap to ceiling tiles. Check the Resources section at the back of this book for some listings and websites.

Dehumidifiers

Mold will grow on just about any surface where there is the right combination of humidity and temperature. In this atmosphere, mold will grow even on materials like steel, which are not normally a food source for mold. Even a small amount of dust can allow mold to grow under these conditions until the moisture it's feeding on dries up. Most people will say that if you can keep your home at 50% humidity it will stop mold growth. The real magic number is 47%. If you can keep your home at 47% humidity or lower, you will greatly reduce the chances of having mold growth.

Dehumidification is something that should be considered for every home with high humidity. Humidity can be a byproduct of a variety of things, from leaking pipes or roofs, to condensation, to a naturally humid atmosphere in a particular climate. Humidifiers are a major culprit; we have torn out more humidification systems covered in mold than one can imagine. If you have a mold problem, a humidifier will make it much worse.

The best type of dehumidification system to install is a central unit piped directly into your heating and air conditioning system. As of this printing, these systems cost approximately $4,000, installed, and will service about a 2,000-square-foot area. A good central system can take about 22 gallons of water out of the air every 24 hours. If a central system is too costly, small dehumidifiers can be purchased at major home centers or most major appliance vendors for about $180. These units can pull about 30–35 pints out of the air every 24 hours. These smaller dehumidifiers are gravity-fed and usually have a bucket attached. When the bucket is full of water, it automatically shuts the unit off. The unit needs to be emptied at that point.

A Word of Warning About Dehumidifiers

Be sure to replace the bucket correctly, or the dehumidifier will continue to run and the water will go on the floor instead of in the bucket. A client of ours experienced this problem on a large scale. He purchased a dehumidifier to keep his basement office dry. This worked fine, as he was downstairs every day working and could empty the unit whenever needed. Before leaving for an out-of-town seminar, he remembered to empty the dehumidifier and replace the bucket. When he returned home a week later, he discovered he'd flooded his basement and office by failing to insert the drain bucket properly. Not only did he flood his home, but he now had mold.

If you choose to install a smaller dehumidifier in an unfinished basement, you can remove the bucket, hook up a short piece of garden hose to the water outlet, and place the end of the hose safely into a floor drain or utility sink drain. This way, the unit runs when it needs to and you don't have to remember to constantly empty it. Dehumidification is key to retarding mold growth.

As builders and homeowners have become more aware of mold and the damage it can create, manufacturers have produced new construction products, and adapted traditional ones, to help reduce this risk. More and more manufacturers are developing these products, so it pays to do some research if you're planning to build a new home or do some remodeling.

Chapter 11

Maintenance Tips for Preventing Mold

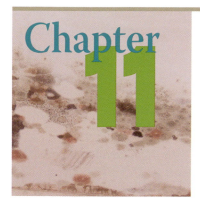

Chapter 11

Maintenance Tips for Preventing Mold

Many people have unknowingly created mold problems in their homes. Common sense is the key in developing a lifestyle and a simple maintenance routine that will reduce the chances of mold and other allergens contaminating your home. Here are some tips.

Flooring

- Consider removing wall-to-wall carpeting if you live in a humid climate. Hardwood, linoleum, vinyl, ceramic tile, or stone are better choices. Mold grows very well in carpet, where it's difficult to remove.
- Use washable area rugs in basements for comfort and decoration.

Walls & Ceilings

- Don't use wallpaper in a humid environment. For a decorative effect, consider a painted stencil border or a wallpaper border that covers only a small portion of the walls.

Closets & Storage Areas

- Minimize clutter, since it encourages dust (food for mold and mites) and makes inspecting for and cleaning up/removing mold much more difficult.

Cardboard boxes don't hold up in moist conditions, leaving items stored inside vulnerable to mold and water damage.

- If your closet is on an outside, poorly insulated wall, it's a prime candidate for mold, because condensation can occur when the warmer or colder outdoor temperatures come up against the conditioned air temperature inside. If you have the problem of poor exterior wall insulation, the key is good air circulation, keeping the air in the closet at the same temperature as the other (heated and/or air-conditioned) living area in your house. Leave closet doors open or consider replacing solid ones with louvered, ventilated units.

- Don't use corrugated cardboard boxes to store items. Instead, use sealable plastic tubs and containers.

- Don't stockpile newspapers, magazines, or paper bags. All are mold food sources.

- If you store birdseed, try not to have more than you'll use in a month or so on hand at any given time, and keep it in a dry place.

- Don't crowd clothing or other items up against closet walls.

- Check regularly for a musty smell or any other sign of mold.

Roofs & Siding

- Check for leaks on ceilings, walls, and in the attic (if you have an accessible one) on a regular basis (e.g., when you replace your air filters) and after heavy rains. Keep in mind that the actual leak may be at a different, higher point, with the water running down to where it penetrates the ceiling or walls below. If you do detect any leaks, have them fixed immediately.

Gutters should be clear and free of debris to properly direct water away from your home.

- If you notice lifted or missing shingles on your roof or siding, have a contractor make the repairs as soon as possible.

- Make sure your sprinkler system is not spraying your siding or foundation—especially if it's on an automatic timer and you're not usually there to see it.

- Don't stack wood or store piles of mulch or compost up against the house or garage.
- If you see algae, moss, or mold/mildew growing on your siding, clean it off with a stiff brush (or power-washer) and an environmentally safe detergent.
- Check your gutters and downspouts and the position of splash blocks and extensions to make sure they're clean and free of leaves and debris, are properly connected, and are draining water away from your home's siding and foundation.

Doors

Keep the tracks on sliding glass doors free of debris to avoid leaks on the inside.

Windows

Wipe excess moisture and condensation off windows to prevent mold from growing there.

- Keep windows closed and rely on air conditioning on hot summer days. A controlled environment means less humidity, filtered air, and regulated air circulation.
- Check your windows for condensation and keep them wiped off, as mold will otherwise grow there.
- Close windows on rainy or very humid days.

Basements & Crawlspaces

- If you have carpet, vacuum frequently.
- For furniture, choose materials that are easy to clean and not porous or absorbent (in other words, not upholstered with fabrics). Leather, wood, plastic, and metal are easily cleaned and can help you minimize contaminants. Consider metal or plastic for items like bookcases and tables in these spaces.

While this driveway is sloped to carry rain water away from the downspout, the small but steady hose leak can cause foundation damage by keeping the area constantly wet.

- Make sure wood furniture in basements is finished on all sides. (Clean, then varnish or shellac, unfinished backs or undersides of tables, chests, etc.)

- Keep the foundation dry by turning off hoses when not in use and checking for leaks at outdoor faucets. Make sure hoses are not dripping water next to the foundation. Drain and store them in winter.

- Inspect for and have any foundation cracks repaired.

- Seal the concrete or cinderblock walls with a waterproofing material. (See Chapter 10 for more on waterproofing basements and crawlspaces.)

- Select mold-resistant storage containers, like plastic bins, and position them so they get air circulation.

- Use a dehumidifier if the relative humidity is above 50% and empty the receptacle daily (or install a hose to drain it outside, away from the foundation).

- Check crawlspaces once a month if possible for excess moisture and/ or mold. If you've installed a plastic sheeting barrier over a dirt floor, check to make sure there's no standing water on top of the sheeting which could indicate a leak from above or below it. Either situation can lead to mold growth.

- Keep basement walls clean and dust-free.

- If your washing machine or hot water heater is in the basement, make sure you have enough light in the area and check to see if any water has leaked around or under the unit.

Decks & Porches

Moldy decking can be cleaned with a pressure washer, but it's vital that

the wood be allowed to dry thoroughly afterward, before you apply a fungicide and sealer. Consult your paint dealer and the product manufacturer's instructions, watch the weather forecast, and plan accordingly. Also check the flashing where the deck connects to the house at least once a year.

While it is not mold, algae can grow on decks where moisture is a problem. The deck should be power-washed, dried, and sealed.

Heating & Air Conditioning

- Use filters rated MERV 6 or better and replace them regularly, according to your air conditioning/heating contractor's and manufacturer's recommendations, which usually vary from every two months—to every new season—to twice a year.

- Check air vents and baseboard fans at floor level in kitchens and baths to make sure food, moisture, and debris are not collecting in them.

- Make sure air conditioning drip pans are clean, and that drainage has no obstructions.
- Have central air conditioning and heating systems serviced by professionals annually.
- Before you move into a house, or at the start of each season, vacuum all accessible vents and heating components—baseboard heating, the area behind and between the segments of radiators, etc.—using a HEPA filter vacuum cleaner.
- Check steam radiators for leaks caused by defective valves or air vents.
- For forced air systems, professional duct cleaning may need to be done every three to four years. If you hire a professional duct cleaner, first check their credentials and their record with the Better Business Bureau, and find out if they're members of the National Air Duct Cleaners Association. The preferred method is to brush the dirt from the ducts' inside walls and use a HEPA or truck vacuum to remove the dirt from the home. Make sure the cleaners have a way to prevent the airborne dirt particles from spreading through your home. (See the Environmental Protection Agency's website on duct cleaning **www.epa.gov/iaq/pubs/airduct.html** for more information.)
- Inspect the outside of your boiler (furnace) once a month for leaks.
- Keep the temperature at a minimum of 64 degrees in winter if you have electric heat to prevent condensation on walls.
- Make sure window air conditioning units are installed with a slight slope toward the exterior. If they're tilting toward the inside of the house, or even if they're level, they can direct moisture into the house.
- Have portable air conditioners cleaned by professionals, ideally once a year.
- Purchase a temperature and humidity gauge for your home. If your humidity level is above 50%, buy a dehumidifier unit and use it in areas of high humidity, like basements. (See Chapter 10 for more on dehumidifiers.)
- If you use air filtering machines, change or clean filters according to manufacturer's instructions.

Clothes Dryers

- Vent your clothes dryer properly—to the outdoors, not the basement or attic!
- Make sure there's adequate space behind the dryer for the vent hose so it doesn't kink.
- Check the outside vent opening regularly to make sure lint is not trapped in it.
- Clean the vent trap in the machine after each use.

Washing Machines

- Check once a month to make sure there is no water leaking behind or under the machine from loosely connected or damaged hoses. Most hoses only last for a few years, so consider a replacement if yours is that old. (Hoses strengthened with wire are more durable than the cheaper types.) If you decide to replace a hose, you'll need to shut off the water supply first.
- Be sure there's enough space behind the machine so that hoses aren't making tight bends.
- If you do find leaks, clean them up immediately and thoroughly.
- Some experts recommend turning off the water supply with the shut-off valve after each use to prevent constant pressure on the hoses.

Water Heaters

- These are a frequent source of water leaks and mold problems since

This new hot water heater has a spill tray to provide some protection against water damage in the event of a future leak.

they have a fairly short life span—usually 10 years or even less—due to corrosive sediments that settle at the bottom of the tank. Water heaters leak when they fail, and they may be located in an area where you would not notice the leak right away.

- Consider installing a water alarm on the floor next to your hot water heater if it's in the basement, out of sight.
- Prevent costly damage to your flooring and baseboards, as well as mold infestation, and extend the life of this expensive appliance with regular maintenance. Plumbers and water heater manufacturers generally recommend draining the water heater—some say every six months, others recommend every 12 months. Follow your appliance

manufacturer's specific instructions, including turning off water and gas or electrical supply beforehand. Be sure that the drainage valve is tight and leak-free when you're done.

- To be on the safe side, it's a good idea to run through a quick inspection of the water heater and plumbing connections and valves for leaks once a month.

Bathrooms

- Towel-dry the tub and shower after each use or spray with an antibacterial and antifungal cleanser, such as X-14® (the original, not the citrus), Tilex®, Lime-A-Way®, and Commercial Zep Mildew Stain Remover®.

- Run exhaust fans after each shower or bath and leave shower doors/curtains open. (If you plan to use a plug-in fan, first make sure you have a GFI outlet to plug it into and keep it at a safe distance from water.)

- Clean up tub, shower, or sink overflow right away.

- Squeegee glass shower or tub enclosures after each use.

- Wash and dry towels, bathmats, and throw rugs often.

- Clean shower tracks (for sliding shower doors) with a bleach solution or one of the shower/tub-cleaning products mentioned above.

A small drip behind a toilet can go unnoticed, causing mold to grow and moisture damage to the floor.

(Use precautions when handling bleach, including protecting your skin and clothes. Do not mix bleach with ammonia.)

- Replace moldy plastic shower curtains and wash outer fabric curtains as needed to keep them fresh.

- Install a triangular waterstop at the ends of tub/shower units to prevent water spraying out past the shower curtain.

- Check the grout between tiles and the caulk between the shower pan or tub and the shower walls above to make sure there are no cracks, or missing grout or caulk. Replace caulk when it begins to become brittle and/or separates between the walls/lip of tub or shower pan. Use one of the new mold-resistant caulks.

- If you have access to the area beneath the shower (for instance, the room or basement below), check for signs of leakage through the ceiling.

- Scrub sink valves and check for leaks under sinks and inside vanity cabinets. This type of leak can cause floors underneath to rot through the underlayment, with major mold problems below.
- Toilet leaks can come from a few different sources, so check the flushing mechanism, condensation, the water supply pipe, and the wax ring connection that is supposed to seal the bottom of the toilet to the drain.
- Have any leaks repaired as soon as possible.
- The next time you have a plumber come to your house, ask to have your home's water pressure checked. If it's too high, it could cause plumbing parts, such as washers, to fail, leading to leaks.

Kitchens

- When you are cooking, turn on your exhaust fan or open the windows.

Mold growing beneath a cabinet where a sink leaked.

- Clean sinks daily, including the rubber gaskets on garbage disposal drains, scrubbing with an antibacterial and antifungal cleanser, such as X-14® or other mold- and bacteria-removing cleaners.
- Check the cabinet underneath the sink for evidence of leaks or mold.
- Check the connections and hose for the sink sprayer attachment.
- Wipe up excessive condensation and spills in the refrigerator. Throw out old and moldy food. Clean the area under the crisper drawers and wipe down the door seals regularly. Make sure the water supply hoses for ice and water dispensers are properly connected. Pull out and clean behind and under refrigerators periodically to minimize dust … a food source for mold. (Make sure you don't dislodge water hoses when moving the appliance.)
- Clean countertops with an antibacterial and antifungal cleanser. Check under the sink for leaks.
- Seal all food, including pet food, in airtight plastic containers.
- Check stove hood fans (which should exhaust to the outside) to make sure the outside flap opens properly and really is removing cooking fumes, moisture, grease, and food particulates from your home, as it should.

- Check dishwashers—all around the rubber door seals—to make sure there are no leaks. Escaping steam or water can cause appliances to rust, and mold can accumulate in the seals and in the surrounding cabinets and flooring.

Curtains & Blinds

- Use curtains made from synthetic and/or washable materials or use washable shades or blinds.

Bedding

- Encase pillows, mattresses and box springs in washable, dust-mite-resistant covers.
- Wash bedding at least once a week in hot water.

Pets

- Dog and cat doors should have a large absorbent mat for your pet's feet as they enter the house. Wash the mat once a week.
- Wash pet beds (or covers) frequently to minimize pet dander, moisture, and mold.
- If you have wall-to-wall carpeting, provide a washable throw rug for your dog or cat to use.
- Clean up water around pet feeding and watering areas.
- Regularly clean bird and small animal cages and aquariums.

House Plants

- Spread fresh gravel on top of the plants' soil to help contain mold growth. Remove dead leaves from the pots. Do not over-water.

Cleaning Tips

- Use a vacuum cleaner that has a HEPA filter and replaceable bags, and removes particles as small as 0.3 microns. Replace the bags and filters as recommended by the manufacturer. (If you're building a new house, consider a central vacuum system, which exhausts particulates, including dust and mold, to the outside.)
- Use a detergent that contains borate—it can help remove mold when you wash clothing.
- Use mold-removing products like X-14®, Tilex®, Lime-A-Way®, and Commercial Zep Mildew Stain Remover® on kitchen and bath tile or counter surfaces (unless it's a type of stone or other material that cannot be exposed to bleach or other cleaning agents in these products). Always follow manufacturers' warnings and instructions.

- Shop vacuums and other cleaning equipment—from brooms and rags to regular vacuums and carpet cleaning machines—can actually spread mold from one room or area to another, so be careful to use clean, uncontaminated tools for cleaning. Filters for shop vacuums are now available with embedded Microban®, a chemical application that prevents mold from growing.

See the Resources section at the back of this book for information on specialized mold cleaning products.

While inspecting and cleaning the various items mentioned in this chapter may seem a little unrealistic and time-consuming, you'll never know what the word "bothersome" truly means until you've had to deal with a mold-infested home. In this case, the old cliché, "better safe than sorry," carries a lot of weight. Seeing your personal possessions heaped into a dumpster and the walls, floors, and ceilings torn out of your home puts these minor maintenance chores into perspective.

In my career, I've seen so many families and their lives enormously disrupted by mold damage. It is my hope that this book can help people avoid this nightmare, not to mention the expense of mold remediation.

Appendix
Resources
Glossary
Bibliography

Appendix

     National average costs from RSMeans' renowned cost database,
     including mold-resistant construction materials and typical
     mold-abatement costs.

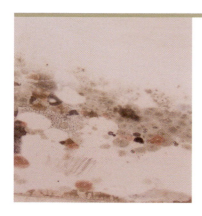

Appendix A
Questions &
Answers About Mold

Q: *Where does mold come from?*

A: Mold spores are everywhere and can remain dormant for years until the right conditions are present. These conditions are: moisture (water leak, condensation, or humidity), food (the material mold grows on, such as wood, paper, and cotton), and the right temperature (above freezing and below 120 degrees).

Q: *Who is at the greatest risk from exposure to mold?*

A: Children, the elderly, and people who have asthma, allergies and other breathing or lung disorders, ARC or HIV infections, cancer, or organ transplants.

Q: *What are the adverse health effects from exposure to mold?*

A: Common, immediate symptoms include: runny or stuffy nose, sinusitis, coughing, irritated eyes, wheezing, sneezing, skin rashes, low-grade fever, headache, earache, and nausea.

Q: *How do I recognize mold?*

A: In 90% of all mold cases in homes and businesses, there is usually a detectable musty or unpleasant odor. Many times you will be able to see mold growth.

Q: How do I know if I have been exposed to mold, and if that particular type of mold is a health risk to me?

A: Have an indoor air quality specialist perform testing to determine what type of mold you have. You can also consult an allergist or a toxicologist to determine which substances you are sensitive to.

Q: How am I exposed to mold?

A: When mold is present in your home or in any structure and is disturbed by air flow or human or pet traffic, its spores will be released into the air. They travel from room to room, attaching themselves to your clothing and household contents. Once they become airborne, you can breathe and/or ingest the spores.

Q: How long after a water leak or flooding does it take for mold to start growing?

A: 24–48 hours

Q: What type of mold infestation can I clean up myself, and when do I have to call in a professional mold remediator?

A: If the mold is confined to ten square feet or less, has not entered your heating and air conditioning system, and is not accompanied by flooded conditions that penetrate the walls and other materials— and if you have no asthma or sensitivities to mold—you can do it yourself, provided you use precautions, such as wearing a face mask, eye protection, and protective clothing.

Q: Is bleaching and painting over a wall an effective treatment for removing mold?

A: No. The mold must be removed from the material or it will grow back through the paint in a few weeks or months.

Appendix B
Health Effects from Exposure to Specific Types of Household Mold

Mold grows in many colors and shapes. While terms like "black mold" and "toxic mold" catch the eye of the press, molds in every color should be of some concern to you in regards to your family's health.

Penicillium/Aspergillus

These groups of fungi are considered to be common indoor molds. They are found in homes in large concentrations after a water intrusion event. They are common in soil, cellulose products, and contaminated foodstuffs. The symptoms of this type of mold exposure are as follows:

- Bronchospasms
- Edema
- Pulmonary emphysema
- Pneumonitis
- Sneezing
- Coughing
- Low-grade fever
- Headaches

Chaetomium

This is a highly aggressive fungus. It will grow on drywall and most anything containing cellulose. It also grows extremely well on leather products. No diseases have been directly linked to this fungus, but it can quickly overrun your home.

Cladosporium

This is by far the most common fungus. It is found on dead leaves, cut grass, straw, wood, soil, and dead plants, and can grow on drywall, plywood, and other surfaces. This fungus has been linked to:

- Bronchospasms
- Edema
- Pulmonary emphysema
- Skin rashes
- Eye irritation

Curvularia

This fungus can be found on drywall, furniture, carpet, and clothing. Like all fungi, it is an opportunist. Curvularia has been linked to the following adverse health conditions:

- Sinusitus
- Corneal infections
- Mycetoma
- Infections corresponding to compromised immune systems

Other common mold spores you may see on a laboratory report:

- Perconia
- Basidospores
- Alternaria
- Epicoccum
- Cercospora

Your reaction to certain molds may vary based on your own immune system. A species of mold that might make another person very ill may not affect you whatsoever, and vice versa.

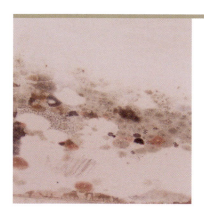

Appendix C
Typical Costs for Mold Testing & Remediation, and Mold-Resistant Construction Materials

RSMeans is the foremost source of construction cost data in the United States and Canada. RSMeans cost data is used by architects and engineers, construction cost estimators, contractors, insurance agencies, and homeowners—anyone interested in pricing construction projects. The costs presented here are from *RSMeans Building Construction Cost Data 2006*, and are based on national averages. These costs will give you an idea of what professionals may charge for several mold remediation-related services. Keep in mind, however, that every situation is different, and the estimates you get from local remediation contractors may differ significantly. A professional in your area may charge more or less for these services depending on the extent of work your specific job requires, working conditions at your home, and labor availability, as well as material prices and other factors.

The costs presented here are per unit (square foot, cubic yard, each item, etc.) and include materials, labor, and any necessary equipment, together with an added percentage for the contractor's overhead and profit.

Initial Procedures

Initial Inspection

For an average 3-bedroom home	$260
For an average 5-bedroom home	$360

Testing

Air sample test	$260 each
Swab sample test	$155 each
Tape sample test	$155 each
Post-remediation test	$260 each

Mold Abatement Plan

For an average 3-bedroom home	$1,275
For an average 5-bedroom home	$1,550

Containment & Preparation of Mold-Contaminated Areas

Pre-clean with a HEPA-rated vacuum and wet wipe $0.35 per SF

Construct a barrier to separate mold-contaminated area from non-contaminated areas. (Assume the barrier is built of 2 x 4 studs, 16″ on center [OC], with ½″ plywood covering each side.)

8′ high:	$3.59 per SF
12′ high:	$4.31 per SF
16′ high:	$6.10 per SF

Construct decontamination chamber for workers.
(Assume it's built of 2 x 4 studs, 16″ OC with ¾″ plywood covering each side.) $5.75 per SF

Cover surfaces with polyethelene sheeting, including glue and tape.

Floors, each layer, 6 mil plastic	$0.61 per SF
Walls, each layer, 6 mil plastic	$0.76 per SF

Seal floor penetrations with foam firestop.

Covering up to 36 sq. in.	$11.35 per penetration.
Covering 36 sq. in. to 72 sq. in.	$21 per penetration
Covering 72 sq. in. to 144 sq. in	$38.50 per penetration

Caulk seams with latex.	$2.10 per LF
Set up negative air machine (1–2K CFM/12 MCF volume).	
	$115 for each machine

Demolition & Removal of Mold-Contaminated Materials

Rent dumpster for one week.	
20 cubic yard (CY) dumpster (8 tons)	$462 per week
30 CY dumpster (10 tons)	$665 per week
40 CY dumpster (13 tons)	$825 per week
Dump/dispose of debris (varies widely depending on the location).	$65/ton
Remove ceilings	
For lath and plaster	$1.98 per SF
For finished plaster, with wire lath intact	$7.10 per SF
For suspended acoustical tile	$1.19 per SF
For concealed tile grid system	$1.39 per SF
For metal pan grid system	$2.77 per SF
For gypsum board	$1.66 per SF
For plywood	$1.66 per SF
Remove walls (non-load-bearing)	
For plaster, lath, and studs	$6.65 per SF
For gypsum board and studs	$2.99 per SF
Carpet & pad	$2.99 per SF
Pipe insulation (air cell type)	
up to 4″ diameter	$4.62 per SF
4″-8″ diameter	$5.20 per LF
10″-12″ diameter	$5.95 per LF
14″-16″ diameter	$7.55 per LF
16″+ diameter	$6.40 per SF

Mold-Resistant Construction Materials & Treatments

Mold-resistant drywall

½″ thick on walls	$1.44/SF
½″ thick on ceilings	$1.68/SF

Encapsulation with sealants

Ceilings and walls	min. $0.48 per SF
	max. $0.81 per SF
Columns and beams	min. $0.58 per SF
	max. $1.22 per SF
Pipes to 12″ diameter, including minor repairs	min. $5.05 per SF
	max. $10.45 per SF

Additional Mold Remediation Costs

The following prices are compiled from the author's experience in actual mold remediation jobs and insurance industry estimates. These price ranges are approximate; the details of your situation will determine your specific remediation costs.

Equipment rentals

Medium dehumidifier	$85–$125 per day
Large dehumidifier rental	$126–$190 per day

Personal protective equipment (PPE)

Protective suits	$8.75–$12.50 each
Protective mask cartridges	$8.00–$21.50 each

Material & debris removal

Remove hardwood flooring	$2.25–$3.50 per SF
Remove ceramic tile	$2.50–$4.00 per SF
Remove vinyl flooring	$1.25–$2.50 per SF
Remove baseboard	$0.26–$0.38 per LF
Remove wall outlet	$1.25–$3.25 each
Remove ceiling light	$15.00–$28.00 each
Remove ceiling fan	$28.00–$38.00 each
Remove kitchen cabinets	$250 minimum or $5.50–$6.50 per LF
Remove countertops	$2.50–$5.50 per LF

Remove refrigerator	$22.50–$35.00 each
Remove stove	$22.50–$35.00 each
Remove dishwasher	$22.50–$35.00 each
Remove garbage disposal	$25.00–$30.00 each
Remove toilet	$28.00–$35.00 each
Remove bathroom sink	$28.00–$38.00 each
Remove bath mirror	$22.50–$45.00 each
Remove tub/shower	$45.00–$250.00 each
Remove insulation	$0.50–$1.50 per SF
Remove thermostat	$12.00–$22.50 each
Remove alarm sensors and main units	$5.50–$22.50 each

Mold Abatement Procedures

Bio-wash	$0.28–$0.42 per SF
Spray encapsulant	$1.00–$2.50 per SF
Clean HVAC unit	$250.00–$350.00 each
Clean air duct registers	$25.00–$35.00 each

The Importance of Estimating the Individual Job

Looking at sample mold remediation costs on paper can be misleading without understanding the scope of work and site conditions for a particular job. For example, access to an area may be very limited, such as a crawlspace 28″ high, or the nearest exit may be at the far end of the home. Often the dumpster has to be located at some distance from the structure due to landscaping or a lack of space.

Demolition costs can also vary depending on the type of materials involved. For example, the time and cost to remove plaster is higher per square foot than for drywall. A fiberglass tub costs less to remove than the same size cast iron tub.

The remediator must also take extra measures, including sealing off the contaminated area, to avoid cross-contaminating other parts of the home. Moldy debris may have to be packaged in vacuum-sealed plastic bags before it can be removed from the structure. These protective steps require additional time, materials, and labor, and are just some of the factors that can affect pricing.

Like all other aspects of mold remediation, it pays to have a general idea of the way procedures and materials are priced, and the types of tasks that are involved. This will help you in communications with mold remediation professionals who are providing you with estimates and work plans.

Resources

This section lists manufacturers of mold prevention and cleaning products, government agencies, and other relevant organizations.

The following list is provided as a starting point for gathering information. It is not intended to be all-inclusive or an endorsement of any particular product.

Mold Cleaning & Removal Products

BBJ Mold and Mildew Remediation Concentrate
BBJ Environmental Solutions
813-622-8550
www.bbjenviro.com

Craftsman Microban®-treated Wet/Dry Vac Filters
800-349-4358
www.craftsman.com

Dupont™ Manex®
888-6DUPONT
www.dupont.com

Laredo® Fungicide
Dow AgroSciences LLC
800-258-3033
www.dowagro.com

Moldex™
Envirocare Corporation
978-658-0123
www.envirocarecorp.com

MoldZyme™
Sorbent Technologies, Inc.
866-767-2832
www.zymoco.com

RIDGID Microban®-treated Shop Vac Filters
www.ridgid.com

X-14®
Wd-40®
888-324-7596
www.wd40.com

Mold-Resistant Building Products

Basement & Waterproofing Systems

Epro™
800-882-1896
www.eproserv.com

Sealoflex®
843-554-6466
www.sealoflex.com

TUFF-N-DRI®
800-876-5624
www.tuff-n-dri.com

Insulation

Armacell
919-304-3846
www.armacell.com

EPS Molders Association
Mold-Resistant Insulation
800-607-3772
www.epsmolders.com

International Cellulose Corporation
800-979-4914
www.spray-on.com

Johns Manville
303-978-2000
www.jm.com

Knauf Insulations
800-825-4434, ext. 8300
www.knaufusa.com

NuWool WALLSEAL®
800-748-0128
www.nuwool.com

PINK FIBERGLASS® Loosefill Insulation
Owens Corning
800-438-7465
www.owenscorning.com

Paints & Coatings

ÆGIS Microbeshield®
800-241-9186
www.microbeshield.com

BioFlex
800-766-9057
www.bioflexcoating.com

EnviroCare
707-638-6800
www.envirocare.com

FiberLock IAQ 6000
800-342-3755
www.fiberlock.com

Foster®
Specialty Construction Brands
800-231-9541
www.fosterproducts.com

SEI™ Chemicals
818-998-3538
www.seichemical.com

Specialty Coatings Company, Inc.
Specialty Super Series®
Antimicrobial (SAM)
800-782-2400
www.specialty-coatings.com

Valprene®
Construction Products Division
410-754-7390
www.valpac.com

Zinsser®
732-469-8100
www.zinsser.com

Roofing, Flashing, & Vapor Barriers

Custom-Bilt Metals
800-826-7813
www.custombiltmetals.com

Enviroshake®
Wellington Polymer
Technology Inc.
866-423-3302
www.enviroshake.com

Fortifiber Building Systems Group®
800-773-4777
www.fortifiber.com

MemBrain™ Vapor Barrier CertainTeed
800-233-8990
www.certainteed.com

Pactiv GreenGuard Raindrop®
888-828-2850
www.pactiv.com/green-guard

Quickflash™
702-614-6100
www.quickflashproducts.com

Tyvek® DrainWrap™ & StuccoWrap®
800-44-TYVEK
www.tyvek.com

WeatherTrek™ with Valeron® EVD Technology
Ludlow Building Products
706-323-7316
www.ludlowcp.com

Sheathing & Siding

Cemplank® Siding
877-CEMPLANK
www.cemplank.com

CertainTeed Fiber-Cement
800-782-8777
www.certainteed.com

ECO-Block LLC
800-503-0901
www.eco-block.com

Nichiha Fiber-Cement Siding
866-424-4421
www.nichiha.com

Quad-Lock® Building Systems Ltd.
888-711-5625
www.quadlock.com

ReddiForm
800-334-4303
www.reddiform.com

XPSA Extruded Polystyrene Foam Association
Insulating Sheathing
703-730-0062
www.xpsa.com/enviro

Wallboard

DenShield Tile Backer
Georgia Pacific
www.gp.com

Flannery MOLD GUARD™
818-837-7585
www.flannerytrim.com

FIBEROCK® Brand Aqua-Tough™
888-874-2450
www.usg.com

Georgia Pacific DensArmor® Plus paperless wallboard
800-BUILD GP
www.stopfeedingmold.com

HardiBacker® Cement Board with MOLDBLOCK™
James Hardie®
888-JHARDIE
www.jameshardie.com

Humitek®
Sheetrock®
888-874-2450
www.usg.com

National Gypsum Gold Bond®
BRAND XP®
704-365-7300
www.nationalgypsum.com

TemShield
Temple-Inland®
800-231-6060
www.temple.com

Walls, Floors, & Ceilings

General Polymers® Antimicrobial Wall and Floor Systems
800-543-7694
www.generalpolymers.com

Kemlite/Crane Composites, Inc.
Wall and Ceiling Panels
800-435-0080
www.kemlite.com

Sonex Harmoni Ceiling Tiles
360-221-7818
www.sonex-online.com

Miscellaneous Products

Ames True Temper Antimicrobial Hose
800-393-1846
www.ames-truetemper.com

DAP Kwik Seal® Caulk with Microban®
800-543-3840
www.dap.com

Sonin Water Alarms
800-223-7511
www.sonin.com

Zircon Water Alarms
800-245-9265
www.zircon.com

Analysis Laboratories

Aerotech Laboratories, Inc.
800-651-4802
www.aerotechlabs.com

American Industrial Hygiene Association
703-849-8888
www.aiha.org

Johns Hopkins University Asthma and Allergy Center
DACI Laboratory
www.hopkinsmedicine.org/allergy/daci/index.html

Northeast Laboratory Services
800-244-8378
www.nelabservices.com

Agencies/ Associations Offering More Information on Mold

American Society of Cleaning and Restoration
www.ascr.org/buyersguide/index.cfm

American Academy of Allergy, Asthma, and Immunology
414-272-6071
www.aaaai.org

American Conference of Governmental Industrial Hygienists
513-742-2020
www.acgih.org

American Indoor Air Quality Council
800-942-0832
www.iaqcouncil.org

American Lung Association®
800-586-4872
www.lungusa.org

Associated General Contractors
703-548-3118
www.agc.org

Association of Specialists in Cleaning and Restoration
443-878-1000
www.ascr.org

Asthma and Allergy Foundation of America
800-727-8462
www.aafa.org

California Indoor Air Quality Program
DHS–IAQ Program
510-620-2874
www.cal-iaq.org

Certified Mold Inspectors and Contractors Institute
www.certifiedmoldinspectors.com

Children's Environmental Health Network
202-543-4033
www.cehn.org

Environmental Education Foundation
480-659-9356
www.enviro-ed.org

The Environmental Information Association
301-961-4999
www.eia-usa.org

EPA Indoor Air Quality Information
IAQ INFO
800-438-4318
www.epa.gov/mold

Federal Emergency Management Association
202-566-1600
www.fema.gov

Health Canada
866-225-0709
www.hc-sc.gc.ca

Indoor Air Quality Association
www.iaqa.com

Institute of Inspection, Cleaning and Restoration Certification
360-693-5675
www.iicrc.org

Insurance Information Institute
212-346-5500
www.iii.org

Mold & Moisture Management Magazine
540-720-5584
www.moldmag.com

Mold-Help.org
www.mold-help.org

National Air Duct Cleaners Association
202-737-2926
www.nadca.com

National Allergy℠ Supply, Inc.
800-522-1448
www.nationalallergy.com

National Association of Certified Home Inspectors
Mold, Moisture, and Your Home
877-346-3467
www.nachi.org/mold

National Association of Home Builders

Household Mold Resource Center

800-368-5242

www.moldtips.com

National Association of Mold Professionals

248-669-5673

www.moldpro.org

National Association of Mutual Insurance Companies®

Mold Update

www.moldupdate.com

National Environmental Health Association

303-756-9090

www.neha.org

U.S. Centers for Disease Control and Prevention

National Center for Environmental Health

404-639-3311

www.cdc.gov/mold

Western Wood Products Association

503-224-3930

www.wwpa.org

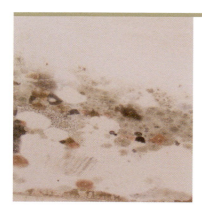

Glossary

AAAAI American Academy of Allergy, Asthma, and Immunology

ABIH American Board of Industrial Hygienists

ACGIH American Conference of Governmental Industrial Hygienists

ACH Air changes per hour

actinomycetes Slow-growing, branching, filamentous organisms.

aerosol Liquid or solid particles suspended in a gas (e.g., fog or smoke).

allergen An agent that induces an allergic reaction (e.g., pollen, mold, or pet dander).

AIHA American Industrial Hygiene Association

allergy Sensitivity to chemical, physical, or biological agents.

AIAQC American Indoor Air Quality Council

amplification Increased concentration of indoor fungal growth as compared to the level of mold in the outdoor environment just outside the home.

antigen Fungi, bacteria, or other toxins that induce an immune response in humans.

antimicrobial A mechanism or condition that discourages the growth or existence of microorganisms (e.g., fungi, bacteria, viruses).

APR Air purifying respirator

ASCR Association of Specialists in Cleaning and Restoration

ASHRAE American Society of Heating, Refrigerating, and Air-Conditioning Engineers

Aspergillus A genus of fungi containing over 100 species, approximately 11 of which are commonly encountered in American homes. All naturally occurring aspergilli are toxigenic.

Aspergillus Fumigatus A fast-growing mold that may cause infection in people who have compromised immune systems or have had asthma for several years. This mold is toxigenic and allergenic and may cause respiratory problems.

asthma A condition involving recurring episodes of labored breathing and/or wheezing. Can be caused by exposure to allergens in the environment, drugs, or foods.

bacteria Small single-cell organisms that can be inhaled or enter the body through food, water, or other means.

bioaerosol Airborne particulates containing biological matter.

biocide A substance that kills living organisms.

biological contaminants Unwanted substances derived from living organisms.

black water Waste water from backed-up sewage or rivers/ponds/lakes that may contain biohazards or chemicals.

borate A relatively nontoxic mildewcide sometimes applied to dry, mold-free building materials to help deter mold regrowth. It is not a permanent solution or an effective barrier to new water intrusion.

BRI Building-related illness caused by airborne bioaerosols or chemical pollutants.

calcium chloride test Used to determine the moisture content in a concrete slab.

carcinogen A substance that can cause cancer.

CDC Centers for Disease Control & Prevention

CEHA California Environmental Health Association

cellulose A material used in manufacturing many construction materials, such as particleboard and wallpaper.

CFM Cubic feet per minute

chronic exposure Long-term contact with a substance or environment (lasting from several weeks to a lifetime).

chronic toxicity Prolonged or repeated exposure to a substance that causes health problems.

CIH Certified Industrial Hygienist

colony Individual fungi growing together.

colony-forming units A term used in assessing the growth of microorganisms on a collection media or air volume sample.

containment Measures taken to prevent the spread of mold from a contaminated area to other areas of a home. Includes use of plastic sheeting as a barrier, disposal of mold-contaminated materials in sealed plastic bags, etc.

contaminant A substance that can have an adverse effect on air, water, soil, or on any other interior or exterior surface, thereby posing potential health problems to a home's inhabitants.

cross-contamination The spread of contaminants, such as mold spores, from the affected area to unaffected areas or people.

cubic meter A metric measurement of volume which is approximately 35.3 cubic feet or 1.3 cubic yards.

culture A technique that allows sample material, such as mold spores, to grow and multiply (in a petri dish) as part of the sampling/testing process.

debris rating A count of the total debris in the air, such as pollen, dust, human skin particles, pet dander, and sawdust.

decontamination Sterilization or disinfection of contaminated areas, materials, or other items to make them suitable for use.

decontamination area An area of the home set up next to a mold remediation work area where workers can sanitize equipment, materials, and themselves prior to leaving a contaminated area, so that mold spores are not dispersed to other parts of the home.

dehumidification A process that reduces the moisture content in the air.

disinfectant A physical process or chemical agent used on objects that destroys unwanted microorganisms.

dry ice blasting A mold remediation method.

dry rot A progressive and slow deterioration of cellulous or other materials under minimum conditions of moisture on organic material.

EEBA Energy and Environmental Building Association

EIFS A siding material, sometimes referred to as "stucco" or "fake stucco."

EMLAP Environmental Microbiology Laboratory Accreditation Program

EMPAT Environmental Microbiology Proficiency Analytical Testing

encapsulants Materials applied to a surface to contain particles.

endotoxin Part of a toxic bacteria or algae that is heat-stable.

environment The external conditions affecting the life of an organism.

EPA Environmental Protection Agency

epidemiology The science and study of diseases in a general population.

exposure Being subjected to substances, such as mold spores.

FEMA Federal Emergency Management Agency

flashing A thin sheet of material, typically metal, that is used on roofs or dormers to prevent water penetration or to direct the flow of water.

French drain A drainage ditch containing loose stone covered with earth.

fungicide Biocide that prevents, controls, or kills fungi.

fungus Organism categorized as a member of the fungi kingdom, displaying characteristics of both plants and animals. Fungi are found everywhere—in soil, air, and water.

germicide A substance that kills harmful microorganisms.

grade The height or slope of the ground relative to a house or other structure. Without proper grading, rainwater can enter a house through foundation walls, leading to mold and other problems.

gray water Waste water from leaking or overflowing appliances (e.g., washing machines or dishwashers) or bath fixtures.

hazardous material (HAZMAT) A class of materials that can be harmful to one's health.

hazardous waste By-products that pose a threat to the environment or human health.

HEPA High Efficiency Particulate Air filter capable of removing 99.97% of aerosolized particulates as small as .03 microns.

humidity The measure of moisture in the atmosphere.

HVAC Heating, ventilation, and air conditioning

hydrostatic Pressures exerted by fluids.

hypersensitivity An immune system response to allergens.

hypersensitivity pneumonitis Respiratory inflammation that can result from acute immune system reaction to exposure to substances (particularly bioaerosols).

hypha, hyphae (plural) A branching structure of growing fungus.

IAQ Indoor air quality

IAQA Indoor Air Quality Association

IERB Indoor Environmental Remediation Board

IFEH International Federation of Environmental Health

IICRC Institute of Inspection, Cleaning, & Restoration Certification. This organization produces many standards manuals for specific procedures in the cleaning and restoration industry.

impactor An instrument for sampling.

incubation Cultivation of microorganisms in an environment conducive to their growth. Also refers to the period of time between exposure to and infection by microorganisms and the onset of symptoms.

indemnification An insurance term meaning to put you, your home, your family, and your property back the way it was prior to any sustained loss as covered by and described in your insurance policy. Also, compensation for a loss.

make-up air Fresh, outdoor air brought into a building via a ventilation system.

microbe An extremely small life form that is visible only under a microscope. Microbes include bacteria, fungi, and viruses.

microbial volatile organic compound (MVOC) Odors produced by active bacteria or fungi—typically described as "musty" or "moldy."

microbiologist Scientist who studies microorganisms and their effects on humans and other living organisms.

micron A metric unit of measure equal to one-one millionth of a meter, commonly used in particle measurement. One micron is approximately 1/25,400 of an inch.

mil A measure of thickness typically used to describe materials such as plastic sheeting, trash bags, or vinyl. One mil equals one-one thousandth of an inch.

mildew Found in the natural outdoor environment, it appears mostly as a white growth on plant surfaces. It is produced by parasitic fungi.

mildewcide A product used to retard or prevent the growth of mildew.

mites Tiny creatures that feed on dust, mold, and shed skin cells. They produce substances that can cause such allergic reactions as asthma and respiratory ailments.

mold A fungi that often has a cotton-like or powdery texture. Mold also produces spores too small to be seen by the naked eye. Toxigenic molds may produce potentially harmful substances called mycotoxins.

mycotoxin A broad category that includes many types of fungal toxins, each with its own characteristics. Mycotoxins can cause disease to humans and animals.

NADCA National Air Duct Cleaners Association

NAIN National Antimicrobial Information Network

negative pressure When less air is supplied to a space than is exhausted from that space, so that the air pressure within that space is less than that in surrounding areas.

NFIP National Flood Insurance Program

NIOSH National Institute for Occupational Safety and Health

NIOSH N95 Minimal-protection breathing mask available at home centers and hardware stores. It should be worn when inspecting for and cleaning/removing mold.

NIST National Institute of Standards and Technology

off-gassing Release of airborne particulates, often from construction materials, such as synthetic carpeting, cabinetry, or paint, that can cause allergic reactions in humans and animals.

organic Materials or substances from plants or other living organisms.

OSHA Occupational Safety & Health Administration

overexposure Exposure beyond prescribed levels–to hazardous materials or substances.

organism An individual plant or life form.

oxidizing bleach A substance that removes color from a material or fabric.

ozone A type of oxidizing agent used to deodorize air, purify water, and treat industrial wastes.

PAPR Powered air purifying respirator

particulates Fine liquid or solid particles found in the air.

PEL Permissible exposure limit.

Penicillium Fungi that tend to be blue-green in color, commonly found on moist, non-living matter. This type of fungi requires less moisture and cooler temperatures than other types of mold.

petri dish Shallow container, usually transparent, that is used to culture mold, bacteria, or other microorganisms.

positive pressure When more air is supplied to a space than is exhausted, creating air pressure within that space greater than in the surrounding areas.

post-remediation testing An atmospheric or material sampling performed after the remediation process to verify that a building and/or its contents have been returned to useable condition.

PPB Parts per billion

PPE Personal protective equipment

PPM Parts per million

pre-remediation assessment/ evaluation The process of determining the scope of needed remediation work at a mold-contaminated site.

pre-remediation inspection An inspection performed by a remediator to verify the remediation protocol written by a third party and defined as a scope of work.

pre-remediation testing A sampling process used to determine current conditions (mold type and spore counts, for instance) at the site prior to the remediation process.

primary damage A term used by insurance professionals referring to initial or direct damage caused by a force such as water, fire, or high winds.

public adjuster A paid consumer advocate who recovers funds for damages for a policyholder from their own insurance company.

relative humidity The amount of moisture held in the air.

remediation The process of correcting a problem such as mold infestation.

respirator A device (available in both passive or power types) intended to protect the wearer from inhaling contaminants.

sampling The process of collecting materials, such as mold spores, for analyses through various media.

sandblasting A mold remediation method. Its disadvantages include the potential to damage construction materials and to introduce moisture.

saprophyte Fungi or plants that live on dead and decaying matter.

SAS Surface air system sampler

SBS/Sick Building Syndrome A condition where a significant proportion of a building's occupants experience symptoms caused by indoor air pollutants.

scope of work A work plan or protocol for a remediation project.

slit to agar sampler A vacuum-operated air sampling device that allows for the growth (and then identification) of cultures.

soda blasting A mold remediation method that uses baking soda to dislodge mold, dirt, and bacteria from materials such as structural framing members without damaging the wood.

spore A small mold or bacteria particle capable of growing into a reproductive mold organism, given the right conditions (humidity, temperature, and a food source, such as dust).

spore trap test Test method that most accurately shows the number and type of airborne mold spores in a specific area.

sporicide An agent that can control or destroy microbial spores that might otherwise germinate into bacteria or fungi.

Stachybotrys Chartarum A greenish or black mold. A product of prolonged water damage involving exposure to cellulose materials. Stachybotrys molds produce mycotoxins considered to be extremely hazardous.

static pressure A balanced condition where equal amounts of air are supplied and exhausted from a space.

substrate A construction material such as plywood, under finished flooring.

swab test A method generally used to detect mold and to determine what types of mold are present.

tape slide test A method used to determine what types of mold are present.

thermophilic Organisms that prefer a temperature above 37 degrees Celsius.

toxigenic Having the potential to produce one or more compounds hazardous to humans or animals.

toxin A poisonous substance.

underlayment Plywood or other engineered wood panels used as a subfloor under finished flooring and as part of the roof and wall structure of a house.

vapor barrier A coating or material through which moisture cannot easily pass.

virus A parasitic microscopic organism that cannot reproduce independently without a living host cell.

visual inspection Evaluation of a structure for the presence of contaminated material prior to, during, and at the end of a remediation project.

water activity The available water for microorganism growth on a surface.

WHO World Health Organization

Bibliography

Building Construction Cost Data. RSMeans, 2006.

Federal Emergency Management Agency. http://www.fema.gov

Green Home Building Guidelines. "Indoor Environmental Quality."

IICRC S520 Standard and Reference Guide for Professional Mold Remediation. IICRC, 2003.

Industrial News Update, Construction and Building. "How to Build a Mold-Safe Home or Commercial Building." Feb. 2005. http://www.industrialnewsupdate.com/archives/2005/02/how_to_build_a.php

Lillard-Roberts, Susan. "Mycotoxin List." Oct. 3, 2004. http://www.mold-help.org/content/view/457/

May, Jeffrey C. and Connie L. May. *The Mold Survival Guide for Your Home and Your Health.* Johns Hopkins University Press, 2004.

National Association of Home Builders. http://www.nahbrc.org/greenguidelines/userguide_indoor_moisture.html

Pinto, Michael and David Janke. *Fungal Contamination: A Comprehensive Guide for Remediation.* ASCR and Wonder Makers Environmental, 2001.

Residential & Light Commercial Construction Standards, 2nd ed. RSMeans, 2002.

St. Paul Fire & Marine Insurance Company. "Mold in Construction Checklist." Feb. 2003. Accessed from eLCOSH, 2006. http://www.cdc.gov/elcosh/docs/d0500/d000512/d000512.html

U.S. Centers for Disease Control & Prevention, Environmental Hazards and Health Effects–Mold. www.cdc.gov/mold

U.S. Environmental Protection Agency, Indoor Air–Mold. www.epa.gov/mold

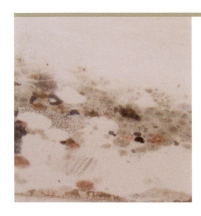

Index